PRAISE FOR

HOW TO GET AHEAD

What a solid tome about how to get ahead in this new world. Times are very much changing. People who are stuck in the old way will perish and in their place will stand people who understand and manipulate the fundamental idea expressed in this book: the future is about your ability to connect with people, sell your skills, and hustle. In this new world, no one gives you anything, but you are free to have whatever you want--provided you do the real work, take chances, and hustle. I can't recommended this book enough.

—Ed Latimore,
author, entrepreneur, boxer,
and personal branding expert

Slayback is one of the sharpest people I've ever met, and one of the few people who has figured out how to break into places you want to be when you don't have history to show you're valuable. Perhaps one of the most important skills in this day and age is the ability to break in and provide value quickly, and Slayback knows exactly how to do that, and at scale.

—Austen Allred,
CEO & cofounder, Lambda School

Until I read *How to Get Ahead* I had pretty much given up on career and personal development books—all generalities and fluff, and no real strategy or specific steps for the reader. Zak Slayback's work is just the opposite: full of brilliant insight and actionable content, and it can genuinely take you to the proverbial next level if you implement it. If your comfort zone has become a prison and you're ready for a jailbreak, read *How to Get Ahead* and open that new chapter in your life without delay.

—Tom Woods,
New York Times bestselling author and
host of "The Tom Woods Show"

Zak's work is insightful, charming, and ahead of its time. *How to Get Ahead* is a beacon for those who have a story to share and those still trying to find their voice. Zak brings back the beauty of communication that tends to get lost in our current digital landscape.

—CYNTHIA JOHNSON,
CEO, Bell-Ivy and author of
Platform: The Art and Science of Personal Branding

Slayback orients his readers towards developing a relentless value creation perspective while giving them nuts-and-bolts suggestions for how to achieve goals worth pursuing. As the child of working-class parents with no connections, I had to discover much of what he recommends here over the course of decades. Whether you are a parent, a mentor, or an educator, give this book to every young person you know. It is likely to be more valuable for career success than are most degrees—at a tiny fraction of the cost.

—MICHAEL STRONG,
Founder, Academy of Thought and Industry

The shelves are full of career-related advice books—mostly boring, repetitive, superficial, and loaded with cheap shortcuts. Now comes Zak Slayback with a refreshing approach that applies keen insights to building your brand, creating a valuable network, and becoming a sought-after professional. *How to Get Ahead* is a road map for personal success.

—LAWRENCE REED,
President Emeritus, Foundation for Economic Education

Throughout his career, Slayback has developed unique insights into how our society operates—learning what works and what doesn't. With this book, Zak has operationalized his philosophy into an easy-to-understand system. The key to success, we learn, is not "checking boxes" or taking life "hacks." Rather, Zak will teach you to build your personal brand, and staff your very own cabinet of role models. I highly recommend that students of all ages read this book, and learn how to get ahead.

—JOSH BLACKMAN,
Associate Professor of Law, South Texas College of Law

Zak Slayback is not one to mince words, and he is also not afraid of presenting ideas that challenge the status quo. I really enjoyed *How to Get Ahead*, but the chapter on execution specifically spoke to me. As an entrepreneur who has only been at it for less than a year, I have struggled with time management, analysis paralysis, and poor habits that have crippled me. This book provided me some great tools to conquer new projects, manage my time better, and build a world class network that has led to some profound opportunities. I highly recommend this book to anyone who wants to narrow down the focus, identify who can help you reach your goals, work smarter and most importantly, be successful.

—DANNY VEGA,
the "Ketogenic Athlete"

How To Get Ahead is an essential read for any individual seeking distinction and definition. Where other "self improvement" and entrepreneurial books fall flat with platitudes, and thoroughly out of touch advice for the less-resourced, Zak artfully and frankly synthesizes steps for personal development, strategies to cut through a noisier and noisier landscape and be heard. It is one thing to affirm to yourself in the mirror that your aspirations are within reach- it is another thing to execute that belief with self-confidence with finesse.

—JANETT LIRIANO,
startup executive, founder, and *Forbes 30 Under 30*

how to get AHEAD

how to get AHEAD

A PROVEN 6-STEP SYSTEM TO UNLEASH YOUR PERSONAL BRAND
AND BUILD A WORLD-CLASS NETWORK SO OPPORTUNITIES COME TO YOU

ZAK SLAYBACK

New York Chicago San Francisco Athens London Madrid
Mexico City Milan New Delhi Singapore Sydney Toronto

1 2 3 4 5 6 7 8 9 QVS 24 23 22 21 20 19

ISBN: 978-1-260-44184-0
MHID: 1-260-44184-9

e-ISBN: 978-1-260-44185-7
e-MHID: 1-260-44185-7

Dedicated to
Colton Paul Slayback
(1996–2017)

CONTENTS

Acknowledgments ix

Introduction: Why Do Most Career Books Suck? 1

CHAPTER 1 **Focus** 15

Find Your Focus, Get a Clear Path to Meaningful Goals, and Know Exactly What to Do to Get Ahead

Learn a step-by-step system for setting meaningful and useful professional goals. Learn how to make a plan to achieve those goals and stop spinning your wheels in your career.

CHAPTER 2 **Learn** 39

Shave Years off Your Learning Curve, Learn from the Best, and Land Great Mentors

Learn exactly how to reach out to the three types of people from whom you need to learn. Know what to say to them to make them want to work with you.

CHAPTER 3 **Execute** 67

Focus on the Work That Matters, Avoid Burnout, and Feel Confident About Tackling Any New Project

Learn a reliable way to prevent burnout and get all of your big projects done without massively changing your habits.

CHAPTER 4 **Signal** 91

Unleash a Personal Brand that Grows Your Network, Brings You Opportunities, and Makes the Right People Want to Work with You

This chapter is split into two parts. Read the first half to figure out how to establish a personal brand online. Read the second half to learn advanced tactics for growing your personal brand.

ACKNOWLEDGMENTS

My students and clients deserve all the respect in the world for trusting me and applying these concepts in their careers. Declan Wilson, AJ Goldstein, Elizabeth Erenberg, Brian Tormey, Simon Fraser, Tim Hedberg, Walcott Denison IV, and countless others were instrumental in helping me solidify these concepts over the past few years.

Lacey Peace and Dylan Langlois are two of the best, hardest-working young people I've ever worked with, and I am grateful for them. These ideas would not be this refined today if it were not for their help and support.

This book is the culmination of years spent learning from people more experienced and smarter than myself. I'm grateful to all of them for the opportunities they've given me and what I've learned from them.

In particular, this book would not be possible without my own Cabinet of Models—the men and women from whom I've been blessed to learn. I'm grateful to my mentors: Josh Blackman (JoshBlackman.com), Dr. Adrienne Martin (AdrienneMartin.org), Alexander McCobin (McCobin.com), Isaac Morehouse (IsaacMorehouse.com), T.K. Coleman (TKColeman.com), Danielle Strachman, and Michael Gibson (1517fund.com).

I've had too many teachers to count over the years—both personally and vicariously through my studies and research—but many of the concepts in this book were solidified through the help of Marc Aarons (8020solutions.co) and Tanya Thomas (tanyathomascoaching.com).

Advisors like Ramit Sethi (iwillteachyoutoberich.com and growthlab.com) and Peter Thiel (thielcapital.com) push me to be definite and ambitious in my own ambitions. I would not be writing this today without them.

I'm grateful to the friends and acquaintances who let me use them as success stories in the book—in particular, Aaron Watson, Ed Latimore, Sol Orwell (and Tam Pham, who introduced us), Nat Eliason, Hannah Phillips, Kelly Hackmann, Vanessa Musi, Haley Hoffman Smith, and countless others. I'm also grateful to those who helped me bounce ideas—in particular, Joshua Fischer and Madison Kanna.

This entire book is a product of the steps outlined inside. My agent, Leila Campoli, approached me after seeing some of my guest posts on Medium. I was astonished by how helpful and effective she was at the book proposal process. She landed me a fantastic editor and team at McGraw-Hill, with Cheryl Ringer. I'm grateful to both of them and their teams.

INTRODUCTION

Why Do Most Career Books Suck?

Most books about careers, networking, and especially "personal branding" suck.

The advice tends to come from two types of people: box-checkers and hacks.

Box-checkers peddle the same old advice you've heard for years since your high school guidance counselors. They write books on "the next big career trends" and guides on rewriting your résumé.

Most of these people haven't had to find a job since before the Great Recession. Some simply republish the same old advice that worked in the 80s and 90s. Or maybe it's recycled advice that worked for them personally. No matter the case, it's likely they haven't actually had to help real people with their careers in years.

Following their advice ends up placing you in a cycle of getting more credentials and checking more boxes as the workplace and market become more competitive. It's fine if you want something really basic, but because everybody else is following the same advice, it doesn't really help you get ahead.

Box-checkers tell you the "right" credentials and how to land the "right" internships. They tell you how to format your résumé the "right" way, go to the "right" networking events, and read the "right" books. Maybe you'll even land the "right" jobs through it all. But you'll feel like you're spinning your wheels. You won't feel like you're actually in control of your career. You'll feel like you're just, well, checking boxes.

This is what happens when you only listen to the box-checkers. It drives ambitious people crazy because they know they can do better but the box-checking advice doesn't really help set them apart.

• • •

Hacks sit at the other end of the spectrum. They know great tricks and shortcuts for doing a few specific tasks in your career. Read their blogs and books and listen to their podcasts when you want to find a quick shortcut for getting some work done or learn how to wake up at 3:30 a.m. every day while fasting.

Hacks are fun and entertaining, but they rarely provide a *system* for succeeding in your career. Listening to a thousand audiobooks on 3× speed in a year won't bring you a group of mentors and models you can learn from and who support you. Taking a cold shower every morning and only eating figs won't give you the confidence to pitch yourself for any dream job. All the tips and tricks in the world won't help you set yourself up for long-term success—only you can do that with a process that is created with *you* in mind.

Imagine knowing every interview, application, promotion, sales, and networking hack out there and still feeling rushed and anxious about your career. You go to your job knowing you can do more fulfilling work and earn more, but you are so *overwhelmed* by hacks, tips, and tricks that you don't know where to start.

It's no coincidence that *hack* means both "a shortcut" *and* "a poorly trained practitioner."

You don't need hacks. You don't need *this-one-WEIRD trick!*

You also don't need somebody telling you to check *these* boxes or take *these* classes and rewrite your résumé to land your dream career opportunities.

You need a career *system*.

You need a career system that helps you find your focus at work, that lets you learn from masters, and that brings opportunities to you. You need a career system that gives you tools to demolish barriers at work, build a world-class network, and feel confident about your career trajectory. You need a career system that helps you build a reputation as somebody others *love* to work with and to whom they want to bring opportunities.

That's the career system I'll teach you in this book.

WHAT CAREER ADVICE THAT DOESN'T SUCK SHOULD DO FOR YOU

Great career advice should help you hit meaningful professional goals. It should help you get that promotion, land that dream job, earn that bonus, start that side business, or close that deal.

You need a strong network to achieve these goals. Most hires happen based on referrals, most sales close from relationships, and most amazing opportunities happen because somebody thought of you.

Building that network takes more than just going to networking events, handing out business cards, and hoping for an introduction. You don't want to know everybody. You want to know *the right people*.

You can build that network through unleashing a personal brand. Personal brands aren't just for Instagram celebrities and people running ads on YouTube in front of rented sports cars. A personal brand is a tool. It's a tool that brings opportunities to you by signaling what you're good at and why people should work with you.

It's how people know to send their connections your way. It's how you build up the social capital and rapport to get top-tier introductions. It's how you meet mentors and teachers and learn from them. It's how you launch your business that lets you quit your job—or gain the expertise and standing to land a lofty promotion at your job. It's how you take control of your career.

WHAT THIS BOOK WILL DO FOR YOU

This book teaches you how to build a personal brand based on your professional goals. You'll walk away with a clear path to bringing new career opportunities to you. The people in the success stories and examples you'll read in this book unleashed their career potential because they applied the principles laid out in this book. You'll learn how different people launched six-figure side businesses, landed their dream jobs, became leaders in their fields, and got promotions they only dreamed of before.

In the six chapters of this book, you will:

- **Find your focus and set professional goals to build toward.** You'll create a map from where you are to the achievement of those goals. You'll know exactly what to do so you don't feel like you're spinning your wheels.
- **Learn how to approach experts and land mentors you admire.** You'll build out your own cabinet of role models who help you get to your professional goals faster.
- **Demolish barriers to your productivity** with a no-frills system to get what matters done at work—without burning out.
- **Craft, position, and unleash a personal brand that you're proud of online and in the real world.** This personal brand works as the core of your professional development. It's your unfair advantage for getting ahead. You can use this whether you run a business or work a traditional job.
- **Land a world-class network of people who can vouch for you and help you get ahead.** You'll know how to drastically expand your network with *the right people* without feeling like a sleazy "networker."
- **Know exactly which opportunities to ignore and which to pursue.** You'll learn how to ethically read people's minds. You'll learn how to make people and businesses *compete* to work with you.

This system comes down to **Focus–Learn–Execute–Signal–Connect–Close.** Use each chapter in the book to master the fundamentals for each and then combine them to create your own Opportunity Machine (Figure I.1). This brings new career opportunities to you.

Each chapter works as an independent crash course in setting yourself up for consistent career success. So, you could turn to the

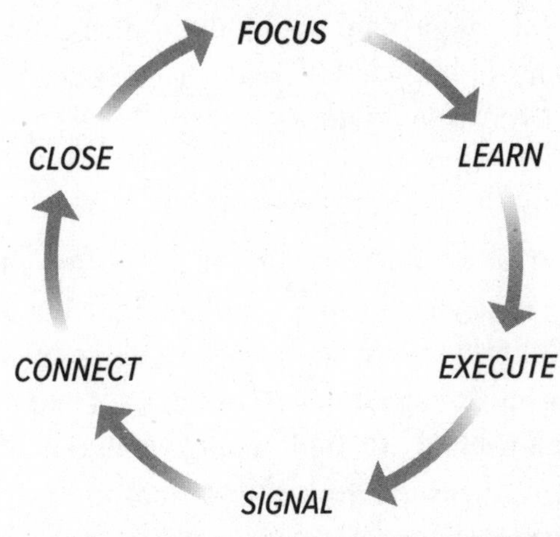

FIGURE I.1 The Opportunity Machine. Focus, Learn, Execute, Signal, Connect, and Close to create new career opportunities.

chapter that most interests you and start there. But together, they form a system through which you can take advantage of what you have now to get where you want to be, faster, with less stress, and more clearly than just checking boxes or plugging through a hodgepodge of hacks.

If you start at Chapter 1 and move through the book in order, applying the Action Items in each chapter, you'll get more out of the book than if you just read each chapter individually.

You can use this system right out of school to land your dream job, in your nine-to-five job to take on new projects and convince your boss you deserve a raise, or to build your own small business or a startup. Like any machine, your Opportunity Machine works so long as you set it up and do regular maintenance.

PROVEN AND REAL-WORLD TESTED

By now you are wondering what qualifications I have to show you this system. I know it works because I've used it myself. I learned it from successful people who used it themselves. And I've taught it to more than a million readers, one-on-one clients, seminar attendees, and those I've worked with for years.

The reality is, if it weren't for this system, I wouldn't be writing this today.

I grew up with an unremarkable background in a small coal town in rural Pennsylvania. My single-parent home didn't come with any kind of world-class network to inherit. The only businesspeople I knew growing up owned a fruit market and the community bank. Through a friend from high school I met the first person who urged me to craft a personal brand. He told me to start a website and write about what interested me.

I used that little bit of a personal brand (I wrote about philosophy because I was a nerd) to help me land a research fellowship with a philosopher once I got to my dream college. The specific subset of philosophy we worked on was moral psychology. I researched how people's emotions motivate them and what it takes to build deep, meaningful relationships in our personal and professional lives.

Then I got to really test the Opportunity Machine.

One of my mentors hired me to run business development for his high-growth startup. My job was to pitch business owners, founders, and executives to hire our candidates. It was a whirlwind combo of sales, recruiting, and education. I met successful people from almost every industry across the United States and Canada, pitched them, and learned from them what it takes to get hired in their industries.

The box-checkers and the hacks let people down. I saw firsthand people graduating from prestigious schools losing out for jobs and promotions to dropouts who signaled the right traits. Credentials only mattered so far as they signaled some basic traits of candidates. Those credentials could be supplemented or replaced altogether with a strong enough personal brand, network, and portfolio. Even for executive jobs.

Hundreds of placements later and after speaking to thousands of attendees in seminars and workshops, I reverse-engineered what worked and what didn't.

I tested it first on myself, then with one-on-one clients, and then in workshops to professional organizations, universities, and students. We landed dream jobs, started side businesses that let people pursue what they wanted, and flooded inboxes with new, interesting, and lucrative opportunities. Now working in venture capital, I get to teach it to founders and professionals looking to succeed in the startup world.

You'll meet some of these clients and students in this book. You'll meet the business owner who quit his job at a Fortune 500 company to make funny vlogs with his kids, the startup CMO who successfully handled doing three people's jobs at once, the software salesman who confidently exceeded his quota immediately after starting his new job, and the data scientist who built a world-class network in just a few months and landed so many amazing opportunities he couldn't believe how far he had come in just a year.

You'll meet friends, teachers, and mentors who taught these concepts to become industry leaders in everything from entrepreneurship to academia to personal development to PR to baking and even being a digital nomad.

You'll see exactly what principles these people and others follow to get ahead and confidently earn more, get more done, and do the work they find meaningful.

This book is a combination of theory, strategy, and tactics, all tested and proven with real people like yourself. If you've ever picked up a book like this and thought, "That's great, but I'm not anything like these people," don't worry. I chose principles, examples, and success stories that work with real people with real backgrounds.

A Note on Buzzwords and Citations

I *hate* buzzwords. But sometimes they're easier to use than inventing new jargon.

"Personal brand" doesn't have to mean sleazily promoting yourself without any substance. "Networking" doesn't have to mean schmoozing at an event. If you're skeptical of these buzzwords, I understand. I was too. Go into these chapters with an open mind, and I'll show you what these phrases *can* mean and how you can use them.

This is not an academic book. But it is the culmination of years of study and real-world practice. For a detailed list of resources that influenced this book, go to zakslayback.com/book/reading.

"IS THIS BOOK REALLY FOR ME?"

If you're still unsure whether you should read the rest of this book, let me tell you first whom this book is *not* for.

This book **isn't** for you if:

- **You're looking for growth hacks or a marketing book.** I do marketing, but I don't really consider myself a marketer. This book is a *career* book and *professional development* book first and foremost. Your personal brand is a career tool, not an end in itself. If you're looking for a book on growth hacking or marketing, look elsewhere.
- **You're looking for a get-rich-quick scheme.** Most people see the benefits of creating their own personal brand pretty quickly, but real success takes time. Just as any pill that guarantees weight loss in a week is a scam, any book that guarantees career success overnight is a rip-off. I don't write rip-offs.

- **You refuse to put yourself online.** A big part of your personal brand is digital. If you're still uncomfortable with the idea of putting yourself online, you won't like what I have to say about your personal brand.
- **You make constant excuses for your career stagnation.** Sorry, but I only want readers who are serious about doing what it takes to get ahead in their careers. If you make a habit of blaming others, your background, or your environment for your stagnating career, you probably won't apply what's in this book.
- **You're arrogant.** This book is not for the arrogant. One of the key steps in getting ahead is humbling yourself about what you don't know, what you need to learn, and offering to help other people who are more experienced and knowledgeable than you so you can learn from them.

If you fall into any of those categories, please go ahead and put this book back on the shelf, or close out of the Kindle sample. Thanks for picking it up in the first place. Shoot me an email (zak.slayback@getaheadlabs.com), and maybe I can recommend other resources.

This book *is* for you if any of these describe you:

- **You want to stop spinning your wheels and find your focus.** You know it's important to set goals, but you want to set *meaningful* goals. You want a clear path to the achievement of your goals.
- **You're starting a new career or making a big transition in your existing career.** You want to start a business, enter a new field, land your first serious job, or make a big leap forward in your current career.
- **You want to learn from people you admire and shave years off your learning curve.** You're excited about the idea of learning from masters and doing new work, even if this means you have to do less-exciting work at first.

- **You want to confidently take on any big project without burning out.** You know you can handle more in your week, but you're not sure where to start. You just need enough guidelines to manage new projects without feeling overwhelmed or burnt out.
- **You want to build a personal brand without feeling sleazy.** You're excited about the opportunity to broadcast your skills and how you can help others. You like the idea of a personal brand, even if you don't have any product to sell or if you work a nine-to-five job.
- **You want to build a powerful professional network that sends opportunities to you.** You want to stop going to networking events full of salespeople and job seekers and actually meet people who can help you. You want to know exactly what to do when you need to call on somebody. Even if you're skeptical of "networking."
- **You want to know exactly how to close new opportunities**—a new job, a promotion, a side business, an investment opportunity—and confidently pitch yourself.
- **You're tired of box-checkers and hacks.** You want a system that works, that you can trust, and that you can use time and time again. You want to feel confident about your career and see yourself grow.

If any of these describe you, I can't wait for you to go through this book with me. I can guarantee you'll get more than your money's worth out of it. Email me if you apply these concepts and don't see progress.

ACTION ITEMS

We'll end every chapter with Action Items. This book is written to be *applied*. There are few things more frustrating than books that are purely strategy with no tactics—or books that force you to finish the whole book before applying what you learn.

This book covers the fundamentals. I've created a few support resources for the book, including PDFs of tables, spreadsheets, email scripts, and exercise worksheets, available at zakslayback.com/book.

REACH OUT

Send me an email at zak.slayback@getaheadlabs.com with the subject line, "I'm ready to get ahead." Tell me in a few sentences why you bought this book, what you want to get out of it, and that you're ready for accountability in supercharging your career.

Let's get started.

Nothing is particularly hard if you
divide it into small jobs.

—Henry Ford

CHAPTER 1

Focus

Find Your Focus, Get a Clear Path to Meaningful Goals, and Know Exactly What to Do to Get Ahead

Declan felt like he was spinning his wheels.

He wanted a career that let him spend time with his family and build a life on his terms. He didn't feel that way at his job after working for two Fortune 500 companies. He wanted to *get ahead* each day—not just *get through*. Following conventional career advice got him to a job where every day and every interaction felt the same. The job looked good on paper, but it left him wanting more. He knew he could do better.

So, he quit. And he started his own business at home.

Declan's business built subscription websites for brick-and-mortar businesses. He worked with health-and-wellness companies, coffeeshops, and the occasional boutique store selling candles and knickknacks. Business was fine by all conventional measures. He could support his family and still have a little extra left over to put aside.

But a few months after starting, he felt like he lost track of why he quit his comfortable job in the first place. Brick-and-mortar companies are notoriously difficult to sell to. He found his precious family time devoured by following up on emails, cold visiting neighborhood stores, and building new custom sites for relative pennies. Once he finished one project, he had to immediately start another.

So much for escaping the nine-to-five.

Declan launched his business so he could be a dad and raise his sons. He wanted to make funny YouTube videos showcasing his home life. He *liked* what business ownership could bring him, but owning a business wasn't his end goal. His business was just a means to an end—to allow him to spend his time on activities he enjoyed.

FORGET THE GURUS AND THE HACKS

This is usually the point where some coach or guru would come along and tell him, "You need to set goals for your business and career!"

But here's the thing: he *did* set goals. He hit those goals. He wasn't reckless. He started his business on the side while working his previous job, set a goal to earn as much as his take-home pay, hit that goal, and quit his day job. He then set another goal to earn enough to support his family while his wife went on maternity leave. He was on track to meet that goal but *still* didn't feel like he was making the progress he expected. He still felt like he was spinning his wheels.

Declan's story isn't unusual. You don't have to run your own business to identify with the feeling of hitting your goals and *still* not getting what you want. Plenty of professionals set out to achieve their goals only to feel like they're just getting the job done to go home at night.

I can tell the story of the McKinsey consultant who landed his dream job only to want something else a few months later. Or the real estate broker who had hit his earnings goal two years early and felt like, "That's it?" Or the talent agent who felt like his hustle was drying up despite the fact that he was on track to be in the top 1 percent of his field in just a few years. Or the recent grads who could do anything with their careers but feel overwhelmed at the list of choices. Or the software developer who landed a great job but didn't know where to go or what to focus on to get herself to the next level of her career.

They all hit their goals. They all do fine work. They all know they can do better. They all don't know where to start.

These people don't need to "set goals," like most self-help and career development books say. They need goals that push them to where they want to go.

WHY MOST GOAL-SETTING WON'T SOLVE YOUR PROBLEMS

Most goal-setting exercises suck.

They tell you to imagine your best-possible life or your worst-possible life. You're told to think about all the nice things you can buy for yourself or your family. You imagine a fancy car, a nice house, and sitting on the beach.

This is fine if you've never thought about goals before. It can be a useful way to motivate yourself out of a rut. But it's rarely helpful in the long term. It's especially unhelpful for ambitious professionals who are good at hitting their goals.

Most goal-setting exercises make two mistakes:

1. They aren't helpful at setting *meaningful* goals. They tell you to imagine stuff you want, but the reality is you're bad at knowing what you'll want in the unknown future. Meaningful goals should not only motivate you but should be a reflection of your deeper desires of what you do and do not want.

2. They don't provide an actionable path toward the achievement of those goals. Goals are useless if you can't develop a path to achieving them.

ESCAPE YOUR MIMETIC ALCATRAZ

When pressed to set goals, most people focus on what they're *expected* to want. This is called *mimetic desire*, and it's why you wanted a particular job or car or vacation or degree even though you couldn't explain *why* you wanted it. You wanted it because other people wanted it, and they want it because other people want it. Everybody imitates everybody else.

I saw this firsthand in college. I remember picking up a copy of the student newspaper, *The Daily Pennsylvanian*, during my sophomore year and reading that more than 60 percent of recent grads went to work in consulting and investment banking. Not 60+ percent of Wharton business school grads but 60+ percent of *all* grads from the University of Pennsylvania.

Dumbfounded, I asked friends who had started out wanting to go to grad school, or launch businesses, or become writers, artists, or public servants but now wanted to go into consulting and banking why they changed their minds. Most of them said it was because that's what was expected of them. In fact, one friend told me, "Anything less would be a waste of an Ivy League degree."

This doesn't end in college. Entrepreneurs and salespeople set earnings goals without figuring out *why* they want those earnings goals. Academics pursue credentials without figuring out *why* they want those credentials. Professionals start crafting a personal brand without knowing *why* they want to craft that brand.

Everybody does what everybody expects everybody else to do. Instead, identify what you do and do not want out of your career and move toward that.

There's nothing inherently wrong with mimetic desire. But mimetic desire becomes problematic when what other people want gets in the way of what *you* actually want and should focus on. You spend your time chasing what others want without feeling yourself getting closer to what brings fulfillment and feels like meaningful work to you. You waste time and resources you could spend pursuing goals you'd find more meaningful. You fall into conflict and scandal with your friends and peers.

People are also *really* bad at knowing what they'll want in the future. Our values change. Our preferences change. Our peer groups, which influence our mimetic desires, change. Sometimes these change quickly. You move to a new city or graduate from college or start a new job and realize that you don't want what you thought you wanted.

So, it's hardly useful to start goal-setting with asking people what they want. *We rarely know what we want.* We trick ourselves. Mimetic desires and cognitive biases make introspection difficult without some guide or set of tools.

> *Think about your mimetic desires and past self.* When was the last time you made a purchase or achieved a goal you regretted? Make a list of the three most recent purchases or goals that you think of. Are they things other people would desire? What makes them desirable to you?

WHY GOALS ONLY MATTER WHEN THEY'RE MEANINGFUL

Effective goal-setting should do two things:

1. Force you to think about the "why" behind your goals.
2. Build a clear path to help you get there.

That's it. Goal-setting doesn't have to be complex.

We start out this book talking about this because I don't want you applying the concepts in later chapters only to end up in a job, role, or situation you hate or build a network or personal brand that doesn't actually do anything for you. Professional development is useless if it's in pursuit of meaningless goals. Goal-setting is ineffective if it doesn't give you a clear idea of what *exactly* you need to do to get closer to your goals.

Most people feel best about their personal and professional growth when they see themselves progressing toward the achievement of *meaningful* goals.

It's not really the *achievement* of meaningful goals that makes you feel great about your personal and professional growth. If you got into your dream college or landed your dream job, you probably know this. It feels great for a few days, and then it all wears off. Sustainable fulfillment tends to come from the *pursuit* of meaningful goals. This is why *flow states* doing work you enjoy feel so great. It's not achieving the goal that makes you feel good—*it's doing the work to get there.*

And it's not just progressing toward *any* goals that feels fulfilling. You could set a goal of watching grass grow and achieve it every day. Unless you're some kind of grass-oriented masochist, you probably won't feel fulfilled doing the work to pursue that goal.

You want a goal-setting tool that helps you identify meaningful goals and helps you build an actionable path to get there. You need a process and a structure to do that while addressing the difficulty of introspection.

AMBITION MAPPING FOR EFFECTIVE GOAL-SETTING

To address this need for practical goal-setting exercises, we use a process called Ambition Mapping. Ambition Mapping is a set of exercises that help you identify and set meaningful goals and make a practical plan for achieving those goals based on proven tools from psychotherapy, psychology, and philosophy.

The two major tools that we will use in the Ambition Mapping process are *sentence completion exercises* and *backward induction.*

Sentence completion exercises were popularized by the psychotherapist Nathaniel Branden in the late twentieth century to help psychotherapists' clients overcome mental barriers and better know themselves. They're some of the most reliable and trusted tools available today for getting to know yourself. Ambition Mapping uses sentence completion exercises to help you get a better idea of what your specific goals should be. They expose you to some of your strongest intuitions about what you do and do not want from your career. These intuitions set the *context* for your goals. You will rank-order these intuitions in a table. You'll use this table to help you formulate a clear and compelling goal.

Do Sentence Completion Exercises Work?

I personally thought that sentence completion exercises were too "self-helpy" when I first discovered them years ago. It wasn't until I followed Branden's instructions to get the most out of them that I realized how powerful they can be. I found myself realizing just what, exactly, I needed to focus on to become more effective and get out of the rut I was experiencing.

If you have any skepticism about journaling, introspection, or exercises like that, I understand. Set that skepticism aside and go into these with an open mind.

Backward induction is the process of thinking backward in time and is a common tool in philosophical analysis. I originally learned this term from Georgetown University philosopher Jason Brennan when interviewing him about his own career—going from working in a factory as a teenager to being in the top 1 percent income bracket of philosophers—but the concept should be familiar to you. If you've ever completed a maze by starting from the end of the maze and tracing your way back to the beginning, you've used the process of backward induction.

When we combine these two tools, you walk away with a clear idea of what a meaningful goal might look like and a set of actions you can take now by working backward from the goal's achievement to where you are now.

• • •

Over the next few pages, we will follow the six steps of the Ambition Mapping process, which include:

Step 1: Determine what you *do not* want.

Step 2: Determine what you *do* want.

Step 3: Filter your strongest intuitions to help you set a goal.

Step 4: Set up your Ambition Map by ordering your intuitions.

Step 5: Refine your goal to definite terms.

Step 6: Build a practical and actionable path to the achievement of your goal by establishing Milestones.

This process takes time. Go into each section with the focus to finish that section. Don't try to blow through all six steps at once. You'll feel better about the process and enjoy it more if you split it into different time blocks or over separate days.

Let's get started.

Step 1: Determine What You *Do Not* Want—*Via Negativa*

Instead of asking, "What do I want?" Ambition Mapping forces you to ask, "What do I *not* want?"

This way of thinking is called *via negativa*, the way of denial. It was first used by early Greek philosophers and later popularized by St. Thomas Aquinas to answer questions about God and the divine.

Philosophers found that simply asking, "What is God?" ended up giving a bunch of answers that all boiled down to "everything good." This was particularly unhelpful when then combined with the question of, "Wait, is that trait good because it is godly, or is it godly because it is good?" So, they realized starting with a process of elimination was more useful. Instead of asking, "What is godly?" they asked, "What do we know is *not* godly?"

For our purposes, we just want to reframe our question of "What do I want?" to "What do I know I do *not* want?" Start with, "What is *not* a goal?"

This *isn't* to say that your fears should motivate you, but goal-setting shouldn't be Winnie-the-Pooh rainbows and sunshine. You want to think seriously about what could negatively affect your fulfillment. Do you *have* to do work you hate? If so, why?

If you *have* to do work you hate for the sake of getting you where you want to go, your goals should take that into account and help you plan accordingly.

One micromanaging manager can tank your experience at your dream job. An unexpectedly nasty commute can sour the rest of your day. Spending time away from your family or your friends or your hobbies can make you resent your career you'd otherwise love.

Starting with what you don't want reduces the massively stressful cognitive task of figuring out what you *do* want. It places *positive constraints* on your goals—a life lived trying to escape the worst isn't a particularly meaningful life.

So, Part 2 of Ambition Mapping focuses on that.

Start by placing *positive constraints* on what to aim at. You can think of positive constraints like guardrails along a racetrack. It's fine to go wherever you want on the racetrack, just not off the cliff along which the track sits.

Positive constraints also help reduce the role of the *paradox of choice*. The paradox of choice is an effect psychologists and economists document when having more options makes decisions *harder* for people.

I noticed this when I started working in the professional development space and recent grads and young professionals asked me what they should do. I asked them what they *wanted* to do. They countered with, "Well, I don't know. I feel like I could do anything. I have lots of choices."

Giving them traditional goal-setting exercises just ended with them quasi-randomly choosing from a hodgepodge of choices. They weren't much better off than when we started.

They experienced the paradox of choice. Rule out the options that you don't really want, and choosing among the options you might want becomes easier (Figure 1.1).

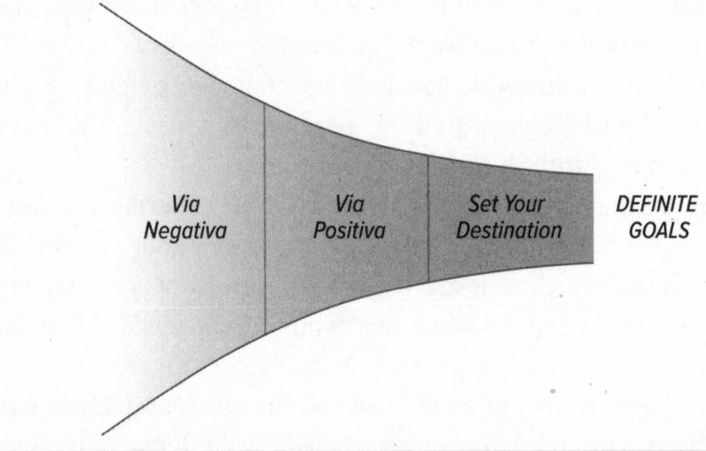

FIGURE 1.1 Think of your goal-setting as a funnel. The first stage should eliminate everything you *don't* want as a goal and push you toward outcomes you might want.

Sentence Stems for Via Negativa

Sentence completion exercises help you get out of your head and focus on the preferences, traits, and values that drive most of your decisions. These exercises are just for you. Nobody has to see them, and nobody *should* see them. You'll self-censor and write what you think other people want you to say if you think other people will see them. Don't stop to review what you have written once you're done with a sentence or check your grammar. Just keep writing.

Begin the sentence completion exercises below by writing down the stem (the beginning of the sentence) each time you write the sentence. Then write *whatever comes to your mind* as soon as you finish the stem. Don't second-guess yourself. If you've ever done free writing exercises, this is similar. Just let your pen or keyboard move with your thoughts.

Do this 12 times for each stem, and do not read ahead until you are done with each stem.

Take out a piece of paper, open up your favorite note-taking app, or download this worksheet at zakslayback.com/book/ambitionmapping and get started.

- I feel miserable when I . . .
- I dread . . .
- I'm good at but don't really enjoy . . .
- I can't imagine doing . . . for the rest of my life.
- I don't understand why anybody would . . .
- One thing that doesn't appeal to me at all is . . .

Review what you've written when you're done.

Next, circle anything that sticks out to you that you don't want in your life *that is a part of your current career trajectory.*

Make note of any negatives that you don't like or want and that you don't currently have a plan to deal with. Don't allow yourself to be blindsided with a negative that might ruin your career for you.

For example, most people hate commuting but don't think about it when planning their professional development. Most people trade a longer commute for a larger house farther away from work. But without developing a plan to minimize the effect of the commute, they find themselves hating their job *because of that one element of their day.*

Or maybe you don't like the idea of working a job that doesn't afford you the security of a 401(k), which your current job does not. But you have a clear path to get from your current job to a job that pays more *and* has a 401(k) plan. Making that clear connection and figuring out what those exact steps are to get you to that new job is the focus of Ambition Mapping.

Most people recognize that they don't have what they want in their careers when thinking about it in passing, but they either ignore this discomfort or justify it. This is uncomfortable to confront. We operate with cognitive biases that make it easier to navigate through the day. One of those biases is *confirmation bias*. Confirmation bias helps us justify objectively bad decisions. Without it, we'd go day-to-day with a stressful feedback loop constantly telling us to reexamine our decisions and make new choices. This is overwhelming from an evolutionary survival perspective.

Use this as an opportunity to examine and confront your confirmation bias. Where do you feel like your career conflicts with your sentence completion exercises? What feels uncomfortable? In what areas do you think you can do better and feel like you're settling?

When you're done reviewing your answers and highlighting any factors you want to consider for your next career move, schedule at least 30 minutes on your calendar to do *via positiva*.

Step 2: Determine What You Do Want—*Via Positiva*

Now that you've identified what you don't want in your career, it's time to think about what you *do* want. *Via positiva* is the opposite of *via negativa*. Instead of asking, "What do I *not* want?" you now ask, "What *do* I want?"

Unlike a traditional goal-setting exercise, you don't list off big, motivating, materialistic purchases you want to make; vacations you want to take; or experiences you want to have. If you're motivated by that, that's great.

But the point of Ambition Mapping isn't motivation. The point of Ambition Mapping is to help you set an actionable plan toward the achievement of meaningful goals. That plan guides whom you learn from and how you craft your personal brand and networking strategy.

Now that you have positive constraints in your mind from *via negativa*, you can think about the traits, qualities, and characteristics you'd like your career to have.

Timing the Exercises

As far as timing goes, you don't have to complete the *via positiva* prompts right after writing your *via negativa* answers, but you should aim to do both within a few days of each other. It's important that the positive constraints from *via negativa* are fresh in your mind. I recommend you schedule a time after completing *via negativa* to do *via positiva within a few days.*

Sentence Stems for Via Positiva

Follow the same format you did for *via negativa*. Write down each stem as you come to it and rewrite it 12 times. Remember, finish the stem with the first thought that comes to your mind. These answers are for *you*, and you should not worry about other people seeing them.

- I feel the time pass quickly when I . . .
- I feel most fulfilled when I . . .
- I look up to people who . . .
- One of the things I've been interested in for a long time is . . .
- I don't want to miss out on . . .
- Even if it is challenging, I enjoy . . .

Take the time to review what you wrote.

Just as you went through *via negativa*, go through your answers from *via positiva* and circle or highlight what you feel most strongly about. What *must* you experience in your career? What would you deeply regret not living out or earning or experiencing? Listen to your gut and your intuitions.

Step 3: Filter and Order Your Intuitions

By this point, you're probably wondering what to do with 144 sentences (congrats on getting that done!). You may feel strongly about some of these ideas, while others look like throwaways that you wrote just to get to the required 12 sentences. Some may even conflict with others. That's fine. You just want to get as much on paper as possible to set an informative, meaningful goal.

Now to *filter* your intuitions. Let the strongest, most informative intuitions guide your goal-setting so you can walk away with a clear guide of your strongest feelings about your career around which you can then set a goal.

To filter your intuitions, return to your sentence stems. Start with *via negativa*. You should have 72 sentences written out (6 sets, 12 for each stem). Look at your first set of 12 ("I feel miserable when I . . .") and search for the *strongest sentence*. Read the sentences aloud and notice your reaction to reading each one. Does it *feel right* when you read the sentence? If no, disregard the sentence. If yes, ask yourself, "Do I feel strongest about this sentence from this set of 12?" When you find the sentence you feel strongest about, highlight, circle, or underline it. Make it clear and call it out. You'll use it later.

How Do You Choose the Strongest Sentence?

You may have a hard time deciding if one is really "the strongest" sentence. If this happens, rank-order the sentences you aren't sure about against each other.

For example, if you can't decide between, "I feel miserable when I commute" and "I feel miserable when I don't know where my next paycheck comes from," reframe the sentences as, "I feel more miserable when ______ than when ______," inserting your answers into the blanks. (For example: "I feel more miserable when ***I commute*** than when ***I don't know where my next paycheck comes from.***") Which feels stronger? That is your answer.

If you still can't decide, don't worry too much about it. As long as the sentences don't contradict each other, you'll get enough context from either sentence to guide your goal-setting.

Repeat this process for all six sets in *via negativa*. You should have six sentences, one from each stem, that you feel strongly about. These should make you say, "Yes! I really do want to avoid these outcomes."

Repeat this process for the six sets of sentences in *via positiva*. When you're done choosing the strongest sentences here, you should be able to look at the list of six sentences you've chosen and say, "Yes! I really do want this from my career."

Now you will have two sets of six sentences you feel strongly about. You'll use these sentences to set up your Ambition Map and set the stage for a compelling goal.

Step 4: Set Up Your Ambition Map and Set the Context for Your Goal

Use your top 12 sentences to guide your goal-setting and make your goal compelling. To do this, you'll need a three-column table like Table 1.1.

VIA NEGATIVA	GOAL	*VIA POSITIVA*
1.		1.
2.		2.
3.		3.
4.		4.
5.		5.
6.		6.

TABLE 1.1 Your Ambition Map. Place your 12 strongest intuitions about your career based on your *via negativa* and *via positiva* sentence stems. You'll write your goal in the middle later.

Take your six *via negativa* sentences and rank-order them against each other. Which do you feel strongest about from that batch? Record them in the order from strongest to weakest in the *via negativa* column.

Jump to the *via positiva* column and rank order your sentences from that batch against each other.

You should have two columns with your strongest, most visceral sentences at the top and your least-strong sentences at the bottom. This should paint a clear picture of what you feel most strongly about in your career goals.

These 12 sentences in this specific order is your basic Ambition Map.

Look at the Ambition Map and ask yourself, "What goal can I set for the next [X] (see below) years that incorporates these 12 sentences?" View the Ambition Map like a checklist. For any goal you consider—whether that's a promotion, a new job, a new business, or an earnings-goal—does it meet your top sentences in what you want to avoid and what you want to achieve?

Timeline for Your Goal

When I've given Ambition Mapping to teachers to use with students or run it with a group of participants, somebody usually asks, "What timeline should my goal be on?" The answer is, it depends.

If you know you want to become a tenured professor in academia and you're just starting grad school, you may have to choose a goal that's probably 10 years in the future. If you hate your job and want to start freelancing, you can choose a goal that's six months in the future.

Whatever your timeline, it should be far enough away to be ambitious but close enough to build a realistic path to its achievement. This tends to be 6 to 24 months for most people.

Take your time with this. Only you can set a goal for yourself, and this is not a straightforward process. Your Ambition Map works as a guide to point you in the right direction so that you don't inadvertently set a goal that you later resent. Your goal should relate to your top sentences as a way of saying, "This will move me further from what I don't want and closer to what I do want."

Doing Goal Research

One of the biggest mistakes you can make in setting a goal is not doing research. For example, if you've never talked to somebody who runs his or her own online business but think you want to run your own, *don't set that as a goal until you do research.*

If you *think* you'd like a specific job, role, or career but aren't sure, reach out to people who have experience with that role and ask them what it is like.

Download an email script for goal research outreach at zakslayback.com/book.

Choose a goal that both motivates you to change your current situation and avoid negative outcomes and is aspirational enough to get you excited.

Write this goal in the middle of your Ambition Map, in the Goal column.

Step 5: Refine Your Career Goals with Definite Optimism

Most goals are fuzzy. It's not clear when they'll be achieved or what goes into achieving them. Compare "I want a job where I work less," to "I want a job where I work no more than 30 hours per week while earning the same as my current take-home pay, before January 31." Which goal is more helpful? Which goal gives you something to act on?

Definite and optimistic goals are specific, measurable, ambitious, reasonable, and time-bound, or SMART. Your goal should meet each of the SMART conditions and follow this structure:

> By ***[specific date]***, I will ***[achieve measurable, ambitious outcome with or without specific limitations]***.

Imagine a goal like:

> I get promoted by the end of the year.

becomes:

> By ***December 31***, I will ***be Vice President of Business Development***.

Or a more nuanced goal like:

> I will launch my business to work from home.

becomes:

> By ***May 31***, I will ***earn in excess of $5,000/month while working from home and working no more than 40 hours/week***.

These *specific* goals include an *ambitious*, *reasonable,* and *measurable* outcome that is *time-bound.*

Ambitious and *reasonable* may sound like they are in conflict. They are not.

Ambitious goals happen on a faster timeline than you likely think they can. Or they have larger payoffs. So instead of saying you'll get promoted next year, choose a goal of getting promoted by the end of the second quarter. Make your goals ambitious by compressing your timeline or increasing your payoff. If you set your bar higher, you'll work harder to achieve that same goal than if you set the bar lower. You should have high expectations for yourself!

Reasonable goals are actually achievable based on where you are now. If you want to become an NBA player but you've never played basketball, it's not reasonable to set that as your goal for next year, no matter what *The Secret* tells you. Sorry.

Consider an example from a friend who works as a VP in real estate private equity. We can take his fuzzy goal, "I will meet our acquisitions goal by the end of the year," and make it SMART:

> I will close in excess of $20mm in acquisitions by December 1.

• • •

Once you've formulated a SMART goal for your career that helps you avoid what you hate and experience what you want, rewrite your goal in the middle column of your Ambition Map and get ready for the final step in the Ambition Mapping process.

SMART Goal Checklist

Use this checklist to make sure any goal is formulated in a helpful, actionable way:

Is it specific? Does it say how the goal will be achieved and by whom? Is there any discrepancy over the definitions of words?

Is it measurable? Is it clear how you'll determine if the goal was successfully achieved?

Is it ambitious? Does your goal feel motivating? Do you get excited about the prospect of achieving it and the doors it opens for you? Is it a stretch?

Is it reasonable? Can you actually achieve it?

Is it time-bound? When will you achieve the goal? What's the deadline? What's the specific date it will be achieved by?

Step 6: Find and Set Clear Milestones to Get You to Your Goals

Most goal-setting exercises get you to a goal and then say, "Good luck getting to it!"

Better exercises ask you what action you can take to get closer to the goal. The best ones ask you to break the action down into realistic habits you can form today.

In the final stage of Ambition Mapping, you use your sentence stems to do backward induction and figure out what *exactly* you need to do in order to achieve your goal through immediate, tiny, and actionable items you can accomplish right now. Whether that means researching more about what you have to do to achieve the goal, emailing somebody who's already done it and asking questions, scheduling an appointment, or simply buying a book, it doesn't matter. As long as your next step is something that is immediately actionable to you, it is effective.

For the next step in this process, use sentence completion exercises again. Your answers to the first few stems may be vague and sweeping. That's OK. You'll make these answers more specific as you get closer to their achievement and learn more about what you need to do. Remember, you're working *backward* in time, so as you go through the exercise, you get closer to present day. You go from actions you have to take in a few weeks, months, or years to actions you have to take in a few days, hours, or even minutes.

• • •

This process takes time and requires focus. Don't do it if you are distracted, and don't rush through your answers.

Start this exercise by writing down your SMART goal from Step 5 at the top of a blank page.

Then, write down this phrase and fill it in accordingly. Finish the sentence:

> In order to ***[insert your goal here]***, first I must . . .

Then ask yourself,

> In order to ***[insert your answer to the previous question here]***, first I must . . .

Repeat this process until you get to an action that you can take *right now*.

Here's an example of this in action: Say you want to earn $50,000/year in online revenue and you already have an audience to whom you can sell. You will begin this process by thinking about your goal and fill in the prompt with "In order to ______, first I must______."

Then, your answers could begin to look something like this . . .

> In order to ***earn $50,000/year in online revenue***, first I must ***sell 1,000 products at $50/each.***
>
> In order to ***sell 1,000 products at $50/each***, first I must ***test a product based on research from my audience.***
>
> In order to ***test a product based on research from my audience***, first I must ***interview members of my audience.***
>
> In order to ***interview members of my audience and do customer discovery***, first I must ***send out surveys to my email list.***
>
> In order to ***send out surveys to my email list***, first I must ***create the survey in Google Forms.***
>
> In order to ***create the survey in Google Forms***, first I must ***figure out what questions I want to ask.***
>
> In order to ***figure out what questions I want to ask***, first I must ***research questions to ask online audiences for product development.***

And so on.

Do this until your answer to "first I must . . ." is something you can do or schedule right now.

Each of these answers will become your Ambition Map Milestones. These serve as a way to track your progress and set you on a clear path to get you closer to your goal.

As you accomplish your Ambition Map Milestones (e.g., building the audience, researching the product, building the product, testing the product, launching the product), you'll get a better idea of what, exactly, you have to do in the next steps. Constantly revisit each step and make sure it relates to a previous step. Your milestones should compound to the achievement of your ultimate SMART goal.

• • •

You've now completed your Ambition Map.

Take a moment to review everything you have.

You have a library of your strongest intuitions about work. You have a guide to what you truly dislike and what you truly enjoy. This isn't just a hodgepodge of feel-good statements. It's actually pulled from your values, thoughts, and ideas about work that you've built over the years and based on qualitative research.

You have a goal that relates to these intuitions. This is a goal that helps you avoid what you most want to avoid in your work and helps you achieve what you most want to achieve.

You clarified this goal to make it SMART, definite, and clear.

You've built a path to achieve this goal with a set of Ambition Map Milestones that tell you what, *exactly*, you need to do to achieve this goal.

And you have an immediate action you can take toward the achievement of this goal.

This is not an easy process. It forces you to come to grips with how you can improve your work now and how little a plan most people have toward the achievement of their goals.

You should be proud of yourself. This is a process you can revisit any time you want to make a big leap, transition, or change in your career. It's the way to chart your ambitions so that the work you do is deeply meaningful. And it's the first step to getting ahead.

DECLAN'S SUCCESS STORY: HOW TO FIND YOUR FOCUS AND START DOING WORK THAT REALLY MOVES THE NEEDLE

Declan looked calm for the first time in a few weeks.

I gave him an early version of the Ambition Mapping exercises shortly after we started working together. He needed some way to get out of his rut and find his focus in his career and business.

He told me the exercises gave him a clear idea of how the pursuit of empty metrics and goals distracted him from why he had started his business in the first place.

"While doing the *via negativa* exercises, I realized that all the stuff I said I wanted to avoid was exactly what I was setting myself up for in my business."

The missing key to his business goals was factoring in the "not": he wanted to *not* work so much that he couldn't spend time with his family.

Declan explained his big reveal at this point in our work, "You're fed this idea that you *have* to work this much, otherwise you're not being productive. But if that work doesn't get you closer to what you set out to do in the first place, why stress about it?"

With this in mind, Declan figured that he needed to earn a certain amount of money and build his business in such a way that he didn't need to bury himself in sales calls for 40 hours every week. While working through his Ambition Map, he realized this meant building recurring revenue in his business, offering services for repeat customers, changing his target market entirely, and hiring a virtual assistant. He saw exactly how he could do that based on where his business was currently.

He felt the world was off his shoulders. He finally had a clear set of goals and a plan for achieving those goals. He knew what he could do, right now.

KEY TAKEAWAYS

- Effective goal-setting is less about having "the perfect goal" and more about setting a goal that you find meaningful and can build a system to achieve.
- Start by asking yourself what you *don't* want and work backward from there.
- An effective goal-setting exercise should give you actionable content to get started on the next stage in your career. If it isn't actionable, you haven't gotten granular enough.

ACTION ITEMS

1. **Find a time on your calendar** where you can work for 30 minutes on Ambition Mapping's *via negativa* exercises.
2. **Set aside your own notebook you can use for these exercises.** You want to have time to focus and get into the flow of completing the exercises for them to be helpful. You can download a PDF version of the guide at zakslayback.com/book/ambitionmapping.
3. **While working on the exercises, don't let yourself get distracted.** Focus on writing down the first thoughts that come to your mind.
4. **Set a time** to do the *via positiva* exercises.
5. **Set a time to review your sentences** from both exercises and research a milestone goal you can set as a SMART goal.

CHAPTER

2

Learn

Shave Years off Your Learning Curve, Learn from the Best, and Land Great Mentors

Most people think that they are at a disadvantage when they set out to start a new stage of their career.

Nothing is further from the truth.

This chapter will teach you why you have an unfair advantage when entering a new stage of your career. You'll learn how you can save years in learning complex new skills and avoid costly mistakes. The reality is that people *want* to help you—you just need to make it *easy* and *worthwhile* for them to do that.

This chapter teaches you how to do this. You'll learn how to quickly pick up the skills and knowledge not taught in formal education. You'll learn how to build a group of mentors, teachers, and advisors who help you get ahead in your career. Finally, you'll meet a few people who successfully got ahead in their careers by applying these concepts.

Top performers all have mentors, teachers, and advisors. They know it's better to spend time and energy learning from those more advanced *now* to save time and energy later. They know to be humble and learn.

LOW OPPORTUNITY COST: YOUR UNFAIR ADVANTAGE

You pay a price for every decision you make. The cost is more than just money or resources: it's time. Every decision you make comes at the cost of *everything else* you could have done at that time.

When you're just getting started in a new stage of your career, the options available to you are likely pretty limited. Even if you feel overwhelmed by all the work on your plate (see Chapter 3, "Execute"), you still don't have the skills, the network, or the ability to engage in all the activities that somebody more experienced or skilled does.

For example, if you want to be a successful online business owner, but are just getting started, you only have a few ways you can spend your time—research, customer discovery, and building an audience. Compare this to the already successful online business owner, who has dozens of responsibilities on her plate at any given time.

As you advance in your career and become more skilled and experienced, your list of responsibilities grows in proportion to your skills and experience. As your list of responsibilities grows, the *opportunity cost* of any decision you make increases (Figure 2.1).

There are only two ways you can gain skills and experience: hope to gain them by chance or learn from those around you.

1. Hope

You could just go through the motions and *hope* somebody notices you and *hope* you chose the right tasks. You can *hope* that what you

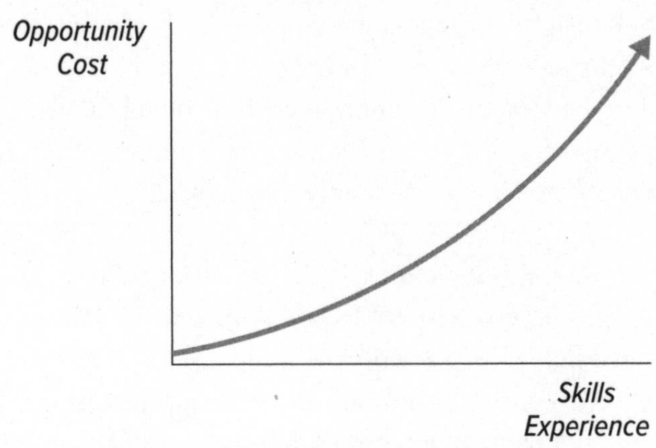

FIGURE 2.1 The value of your time increases dramatically as you acquire skills and knowledge.

learn in formal education translates over into real-world application. And you can *hope* that all the information you take in through study is the right information to get ahead.

2. Learn from Those Around You

Or, you can use your low opportunity cost to your advantage. You can find other people who have the skills, knowledge, and experience you want to gain and learn directly from them. You can pick up the knowledge that's impossible to teach in a classroom and learn it from masters with years of experience. You can gain skills from people specialized in the teaching. You can find *models.*

Models give you a foundation against which you can track your professional progress, a set of knowledge to learn from, and the chance to pitch yourself for responsibilities that help you get ahead.

This is the idea behind the apprenticeship model that dominated professional development for centuries. Professionals and craftspeople starting out in a new stage of their careers would work with a master. The master had more responsibilities on his plate than he could handle, so he would delegate less-skilled tasks to apprentices. Although these were relatively simple tasks for the master, they'd challenge the apprentice, pushing apprentices to improve their skills through real-world practice.

A major benefit of the apprenticeship model is learning *tacit knowledge*, or knowledge that cannot easily be taught through textbooks or lectures. It's gained only through relevant practice and experience. You can study some skills all you want, but you won't internalize those skills without hands-on experience.

Learning a language quickly is a strong illustration in the difference between tacit knowledge and *explicit* knowledge (that knowledge you *can* gain through textbooks and lectures). Imagine studying a language through high school and college and then visiting a country that speaks that language. Despite having studied the language for years, you struggle to get started speaking with locals. But after a few weeks immersed in that language, you'll most likely make more progress in that short time than you did for years in a classroom environment. That's because most languages are governed by *tacit knowledge.* Linguistic rules, norms, and customs develop over time as needed. They're rarely handed down from somebody studying the fundamentals of linguistics in a classroom. If you want to learn any language quickly, spend a few weeks in a country that only speaks that language.

Learning career skills—especially those based on industry norms and soft skills—works the same way. You can read about sales, software development, public speaking, or professional writing all you want. But it isn't until you start getting feedback from the real world and learning the niceties of what works and what doesn't work that you will see progress.

When you don't learn tacit knowledge through apprenticing under masters, you usually learn it through failing and getting negative feedback from the world. While this is better than not learning tacit knowledge at all, it's costly, time-consuming, and discouraging. It's better to take the time when starting a new stage of your career to learn tacit knowledge from the masters than to wait for a random event to knock you down and learn the hard way.

You can get the benefits of learning tacit knowledge from mentors, learning explicit knowledge from teachers, and learning wisdom from advisors. You can do this yourself with a few projects, emails, and persistence, as I will show you in the next section.

ACCELERATE YOUR SUCCESS BY BUILDING YOUR OWN CABINET OF MODELS

Just as you should have great role models while growing up, you should have great professional models in your career.

Professional models do more than give you something to aspire to. They give you access to tacit *and* explicit knowledge in a way that you simply cannot get elsewhere.

Just as a company might have a board of advisors or a politician might have a cabinet of experts, you should build out your own Cabinet of Models for any major career moves you want to make.

But professional models are more than just "people who do what I want to do." Some models are experts in pattern recognition and give you access to time-tested wisdom. Others teach skills you need to acquire and are specifically specialized in *teaching* those skills. And still others provide an opportunity for you to arbitrage opportunity cost and do valuable work they don't have time to do.

Your Cabinet of Models is made up of advisors, teachers, and mentors.

Mutual Exclusivity

Advisors, teachers, and mentors are *general* categories into which professional models fall. Some people may be more than one. You may hire a coach or a teacher in a subject and later build a personal relationship with that person as an advisor. Some teachers may also make great mentors if they're open to working with you.

Advisors: Meet with Them

When you find yourself confused or unclear about how to proceed on a specific goal or milestone, reach out to an advisor for expertise and guidance.

Advisors have at least achieved something you want to achieve and can give you guidance on what they did right or wrong. You may meet with an advisor once over a phone call or many times over your career. Every relationship will be different.

Consider approaching an advisor if you need explicit advice that stems from years of experience in your field or a field you're interested in. Expertise is a function of experience. Expertise involves pattern recognition and an ability to quickly differentiate between good and bad patterns. Pattern recognition comes from exposure to large sample sizes over time. That only comes from experience.

Qualities of an Excellent Advisor

An advisor should have the following qualities:

- **Accessible.** Advisors should be open and willing to have a conversation with you when you need to speak with them. This might be grabbing coffee, hopping on a phone call, or meeting them over a meal. Build accessibility by proving to them that you won't waste their time.
- **Possesses expertise.** Advisors have enough experience to recognize successful and unsuccessful patterns before others can. The best advisors have expertise in their fields.
- **Has achieved what you want to achieve.** Advisors can be domain-specific (they've achieved a goal you want to achieve, but they work in a different career) or career-specific (they currently do what you want to do). What matters is that they can provide direct feedback and advice.
- **Good network.** A major benefit to building a Cabinet of Models is that you can tap it for networking and relationship-building purposes. Great advisors should have a network they can introduce you to when needed.

Time Frame

The time frame for meeting with advisors is variable. You may meet with them once to answer specific questions related to a goal or regularly to get general feedback.

Knowledge Type

Advisors offer expertise and explicit knowledge. *Expertise* is the ability to recognize patterns quickly and give you feedback you wouldn't get from a teacher. Advisors should also have explicit knowledge. They can answer straightforward questions about what they did (or failed to do) in pursuit of a professional goal you share.

Weight to Give Them

Take what advisors say with a grain of salt. People rewrite their own histories and are remarkably bad at knowing the "what if" of alternate decisions. They're still part of a balanced Cabinet of Models because they offer input similar to mentors but you don't necessarily have the ability to work with or for them.

Examples of Advisor Relationships

You want to get your website to the first page of Google. You could hire an SEO expert to talk to you and teach you what you need to do. You could also reach out to a blogger you respect who is on the first page of Google and ask her how she got there, what kind of content she created, and what missteps she made along the way.

You want to get hired at your dream job, but you don't know how to approach the company. Reach out and ask a current or former employee directly how you should pitch hiring managers and to whom, exactly, you should speak.

How to Approach Advisors

The advisor model is the least formal role in a Cabinet of Models. Identify people who have already achieved the milestones you want to achieve (use your Ambition Map if this isn't clear) and reach out to them directly or through introductions. When reaching out, make your questions clear and keep emails to single questions. Don't immediately go for a meeting or call without first establishing why you want to talk to them. After meeting with them, send a thank you email (and consider a gift or a card if they went out of their way to talk to you) and keep them updated of your progress.

Relationship Maintenance Emails

Send *maintenance emails* to anybody you want to keep engaged but have little reason to talk to outside of any meetings or calls. Send a quick message that gives the person a relevant update and might share an interesting piece of content with them. The purpose of the email *isn't* to get a reply—it's to just keep the person engaged should you reach back out for another meeting or call in the future.

A maintenance email doesn't have to be complicated. It can be as simple as this:

> Hi John,
>
> Thanks again for sitting down with me a few weeks ago and telling me about how you raised $20mm for your first fund. I applied some of what you discussed, and I wanted to let you know we just did our first close at $10mm.
>
> NRN - I know you're busy. Just wanted to keep you updated.
>
> Zak
>
> PS - I thought you might enjoy this article on crypto exchange KYM standards given your interest in Bitcoin: ***[LINK]***

Teachers: Hire Them

Have you ever tried to teach yourself a skill and found it overwhelming? Were you confused where to start? Which books to read and which to ignore? Did you find yourself spending more time trying to learn the skill than it was worth?

This is when you should hire a teacher.

A cynical interpretation of teachers is, "those who cannot do, teach." Don't think of teachers this way. Teachers aren't *nondoers.* Teachers are professionals who have *also* developed the skills of teaching and coaching. They may not be *the best* at the skill they teach, but they're skilled at transferring explicit knowledge to students and clients.

Chuck Noll, Steelers head coach from 1969 to 1991, was one of the best coaches in NFL history. He turned the team around from being one of the worst in the league to one of the best. But Noll was a mediocre football player. His skills lay in *teaching* and *coaching* football, not in *playing* football. Teachers need not be the best players.

A client-teacher relationship is a formal relationship where you pay the teacher for his or her time and knowledge. This aligns the incentives between the client (you) and the teacher. You want teachers accountable for producing a result. Good teachers cost money. In an age of free online resources and classes, paid teachers provide an ability to combine experience-based expertise with information distillation (the ability to tell you what to focus on and what to ignore to prevent information overload).

People who are willing to teach anybody without being compensated for their time and expertise are less likely to *have* expertise valuable enough to pay for.

Hire a teacher when you want to improve or develop a specific skill quickly and to a level of serious depth. While you *could* self-educate, self-education assumes you have an ability to easily prioritize which knowledge to pursue. Excellent teachers save you hours by telling you what to ignore and what to focus on. They can also help you identify "good-enough" standards so that you know when to stop learning and move on to execution.

Qualities of an Excellent Teacher

A teacher should have the following qualities:

- **Believable.** Good teachers should have a history of successfully teaching the skills you want to learn and should be able to adequately explain how they would do that. (For more on *believability* in hiring teachers, see zakslayback.com/believability.) Look for endorsements and testimonials from past clients, as well as a basic ability to do what they claim to teach.
- **Versed in coaching/consulting.** Not everybody who has a skill can *teach* that skill. Excellent teachers should not only have a basic grasp of the skill they teach but they also should have a grasp of coaching, consulting, or teaching *as skills*.
- **Charge for their time.** Qualified teachers should value their time and expertise enough to charge for it. Paying teachers for their time also puts *your* skin in the game and forces you to use time with them more efficiently.

Time Frame

The time frame for teachers is the short to medium term. Work with teachers as long as you need to to develop the skills they teach. Hire new teachers as your skills advance. It's rare to find a teacher who can teach beginners and advanced students alike.

Knowledge Type

Teachers offer explicit and coaching knowledge. Teachers are skilled in transferring explicit knowledge and guiding clients to know how to solve problems through coaching.

Weight to Give Them

Give teachers' input strong weighting *in their domains.* Don't weigh their input heavily outside of their domain expertise. Domain expertise is *domain* expertise and doesn't transfer to other domains.

Example of a Teacher Relationship

Serious professionals often hire experts and teachers in areas they want to improve in. *New York Times* bestselling author Ramit Sethi (iwillteachyoutoberich.com) hired marketing teacher Jay Abraham (abraham.com) when he wanted to get serious about making his blog a multimillion-dollar business. Abraham has strong believability in marketing and charges (now more than $150,000!) for his coaching services.

How to Approach Teachers

Teachers may work as part of an organization (e.g., Sandler Sales System teachers work for a Sandler franchise) or independently as freelancers or small businesspeople. If they don't work through an established teaching or coaching system, identify an outcome you want them to help you with and email them asking if they do coaching. If they do, ask for a consultation call and for success stories or testimonials. The combination of their input on your consultation call and the success stories will let you know if they pass believability for teaching.

Mentors: Work with Them

Mentors are any professionals doing what you want to do that you can work with and learn from. Work with and for them to learn tacit knowledge and gain valuable experience that you can then use to get ahead.

The trick to finding a good mentor lies in not looking for a "mentor." Their plates are so full of responsibilities and tasks to complete that they don't have time to hang out at "mentoring events."

Good mentors don't actively think about "mentoring" (unless it's an HR move inside their own company). They have responsibilities and work to do. You access them not through asking them to "mentor" you but through providing value to them by taking tasks and responsibilities off their plates.

Don't Go to Mentorship Events

You probably won't find a great mentor at a mentorship event. The opportunity cost of attending such an event is too high. Instead, you'll find people who think of mentorship as a consumption good (they just think it's fun) or people who don't quite have the responsibilities and experience to mentor you. Don't go to mentorship events. Spend your time pitching an experienced professional to let you work with him or her instead.

The right mentor can accelerate your career by years. Mentors provide an *example* of how to get ahead, give active feedback on your work (and have an incentive to do so when you work with them), and have their own established networks you can access if you impress them well.

Perhaps more important in building out your personal brand as a career tool, mentors provide you a chance to build a portfolio of work and gain relevant experience. When thinking of your career as a system, *prioritize opportunities to create work and gain experience that will help land more and better opportunities down the line.* Taking valuable work off your mentor's plate does this.

Qualities of an Excellent Mentor

A mentor should have the following qualities:

- **High opportunity cost.** Excellent mentors should be very busy and have their plates full of responsibilities and tasks. They should be the kind of people who stay on top of their work (you don't want to work with somebody who is disorganized and can't get work done), but who have to prioritize because they can't get *everything* done. This gives you an opportunity to arbitrage between what they can't get done and what you can still learn.
- **Track record of lifting up the people they work with.** You won't always work with the same mentors. As your skills and

experience improve, you'll want to trade up mentors. You want to work with a mentor who lifts up teammates rather than holds them back for jealous or selfish reasons. Look for professionals with histories of leading teams or working with younger and less-experienced professionals.

- **Established networks and high peer esteem.** Use the respect you earn from your mentor as a way to meet established professionals in *their* network, shaving months and years off your networking plans (see Chapter 5). Look for professionals with their own established networks and who don't silo and isolate themselves from their peers.
- **Accessibility.** It's important to work closely with a mentor so that you can learn niceties that don't come out in a formal teaching setting. Look for somebody excited about the opportunity to hand off valuable tasks and responsibilities to a junior professional who wants to work with him or her. Professionals who are hesitant to work with you don't tend to be good mentors—consider approaching them as advisors instead. See Table 2.1 for a summary of differences and qualities of all three model types.

Time Frame

The time frame for a mentor is the medium to long term. You want to work with mentors long enough to gain relevant experience, build a portfolio of work, and develop a strong relationship.

Knowledge Type

Mentors offer tacit and experience-based knowledge. Work with mentors to gain relevant experience and develop skills that require tacit knowledge. Sit in on meetings and calls, watch how they do work, and be aware of their processes for getting work done (which they may not have fully explicated themselves).

MENTORS	TEACHERS	ADVISORS
You pitch them on value you can create and then work with or for them.	You hire them.	You meet with them.
Give you a network, chance to build a portfolio, and tacit knowledge.	Give you teaching, coaching, skills, and resources.	Give you advice.
Qualified based on experience and opportunity cost.	Qualified based on believability.	Qualified based on wisdom (experience + esteem).
"Do as I did, not *necessarily* as I say."	"Do as I say, not *necessarily* as I do."	"Do as I say, but take it with a grain of salt."
Trade up as your opportunity cost rises.	Trade up as your skills improve.	Trade up as your situation requires.
Tacit knowledge.	Explicit knowledge.	Expertise.
Medium- to long-term relationships.	Short- to medium-term relationships.	Variable-term relationships.

TABLE 2.1 The Differences Between Mentors, Teachers, and Advisors.

Weight to Give Them

Don't look to mentors for explicit teaching. Instead, think of the knowledge you gain from them as "do as I did, not as I say" (or, "don't do as I did in cases where they failed).

Example of a Mentor Relationship

Charlie Hoehn (charliehoehn.com) reached out to Tim Ferriss (tim.blog; author of *The 4-Hour Workweek*, *The 4-Hour Body*, and *The 4-Hour Chef*) between the publication of *The 4-Hour Workweek* and *The 4-Hour Body*. When he reached out to Ferriss, he offered him tasks he could do to help him while he was working on *The 4-Hour Body*. For the next three years, the two worked together and helped launch Hoehn's career as an author and paid speaker. In Hoehn's case, he started with offering free work to Ferriss. While not everybody has the ability to work for free, if you can do so, consider starting with free work. If you create value for the mentor while staying sufficiently self-guided, most will happily start paying you to keep you involved.

I followed a similar process to land my job at Praxis with Isaac Morehouse. I reached out to Morehouse while he was launching his startup and offered to take over content management, email newsletters, and tabling at conferences. I soon took on all operations responsibilities. This let me become an early employee at that growing startup, without any real qualifications besides the fact that I could complete work that the founder needed done but didn't have the time to do himself. I later traded this experience up to beat out candidates who were considerably older than me for a business development position.

How to Land an Excellent Mentor Who Helps You Get Ahead in Your Career

You don't have to hope that you stumble into the right mentor or hope that a busy professional lets you work with him or her. You also don't have to (and shouldn't) go begging for help at "mentorship events."

There's a straightforward and proven way to land an excellent mentor. It stems from understanding their opportunity cost. All it takes is identifying tasks that aren't worth their time but *are* worth your time.

Time Commitment

Working with a mentor can be a part-time or full-time opportunity.

You can use this system to land a mentor while you work to get promoted. Or you can use it to land a mentor who offers you a full-time job at a new company. Or you can even use it to land a mentor with whom you work while building your own business.

Whichever path you choose to take, remember that mentorship looks more like work than it looks like getting coffee and asking somebody, "Will you mentor me?" Quality mentors often balk at being asked to "mentor." They're too busy for open-ended asks like that.

Follow these steps to find, approach, and pitch a mentor who can help you accelerate your professional success. Use this whether you work a nine-to-five you enjoy, want to land your dream job, or hope to launch your own business.

Step 1. Identify Potential Mentors by Looking for Busy People

Start by identifying what kinds of person you need to work with to get ahead. You don't just want to meet with any experienced professional or somebody doing what you want to do. You want to work with mentors who will lift you up.

Look for accessible, busy people working in the field or stage of career you want. If you want to become a professional artist and have no previous experience selling art, don't go to the top world-famous artists. You may someday land them as mentors, but start by working with somebody you can actually reach first. If you are an established sales professional and want to become one of the very best in your field, look for people who are better than you, who are at least a few years ahead of you, and who could use your help.

Ask yourself, "Who is very busy, does what I want to do, has a plate I can help clear, and I can reach?"

Competition Is for Losers

Don't turn to job fairs or job postings to find these opportunities, either. While you can turn your mentorship into a job, the best mentorships come from setting yourself apart from the pack, not throwing your résumé into the same pile as everybody else.

Instead, use a strategy that I tested and proved from both sides of the talent table—at placement in Praxis and as portfolio support in venture capital. My readers regularly use this strategy for expanding their own mentorship networks.

Start with resources like the *Inc 5000 Fastest Growing Companies* list (www.inc.com/inc5000/) or your local business newspaper's fastest growing companies lists.

If you have a specific interest in working with startups, go to AngelList (angel.co) and Crunchbase (crunchbase.com) and look for companies that recently raised money from investors.

Companies on these lists are growing *quickly*. One of the biggest pain points for a fast-growing company is finding enough talent. Approach them when they're growing and they will almost certainly need your help.

They may be senior colleagues at your employer. They may be total strangers. It doesn't matter. You don't have to know them directly right now. You'll research outreach and introductions in the next step.

Make a list of people you can reach out to, what their roles are, and why you want to learn from them. I recommend doing this in a spreadsheet with columns labeled: first, last, email, role, company, mutual connection 1, mutual connection 2, value-add, notes.

Step 2. Identify Potential Ways to Meet with Them

You just need one person on your list to let you work with him or her.

Don't get caught up in networking and relationship-building with a ton of people. Just focus on the people on your list.

Networking and mass relationship-building come into play later when you have a tailored personal brand and clear positioning (as we will learn in Chapter 5). Right now, just focus on finding an opportunity to do great work with experienced professionals.

There are two ways to reach potential mentors:

1. Send an email or message to a person without having any mutual connections (*cold outreach*).
2. Be introduced by a mutual connection (*warm outreach*).

Warm introductions have higher positive reply rates than cold emails, so do your best to start there.

Go through your list of potential mentors and search them individually on LinkedIn and social media sites. Look for mutual connections. Depending on the strength of your relationships with the mutual connections, list them in your document as people who can make introductions for you.

Getting Colleagues to Mentor You

Maybe you want a senior colleague to mentor you. If this is the case, you don't have to get a warm introduction or prospect him or her for outreach. You just need to reach out directly and let the person know that you'd like to solve specific issues for him or her. If that's the case, skip to Step 3.

If you don't have any strong mutual connections with your potential mentors, look up their email addresses. Use FindThat-Lead (findthatlead.com), ContactOut (contactout.com), or Hunter (hunter.io) to quickly find email addresses. Save these in your mentor prospecting document.

Step 3. Identify Problems You Can Solve and Value You Can Create

You do *not* want to be that person who reaches out with an email that just says, "I like what you do! Mentor me! Mentor me!" That screams, "I have no idea what I am doing, and I am going to waste more of your time than I am worth." In the *few* cases where that works, it's because the person reaching out looks like a charity case and the mentor feels good helping him or her. Don't be a charity case.

The World's Most Popular Radio Station

Zig Ziglar used to joke that everybody in the world has the same favorite radio station: WII-FM—*What's in It for Me?*

When trying to get a busy potential mentor to listen to you, ask yourself, "What's in it for this person to talk to and work with me?"

Since great mentors are busy and have high opportunity cost for all of their decisions, make it clear to them that working with you is worth their time.

You're probably wondering what kinds of tasks you can complete that are worth both your time and make them want to give you time. Start by putting yourself in their shoes.

Understand that busy people must prioritize their tasks if they want to be effective. There's *always* more to do when you have skills, experience, and responsibilities. Management gurus often outline all actions as falling into one of four categories: urgent and important, not urgent and important, urgent and not important, and not urgent and not important.

The tasks that potential mentors must do themselves, because they are the only people with the skills and knowledge to do those tasks, are important tasks (Table 2.2). The tasks that must get done *now* or else they can't do their job are urgent tasks. Not important tasks can be delegated to somebody else who is unskilled or less-skilled. Not urgent tasks can be scheduled for later.

In the reality of business, few tasks that get listed as urgent and important or urgent and not important actually get done. Fires pop up. Calls and meetings take longer than expected. And sometimes you just can't hire fast enough to get everything delegated away. (One of the biggest reasons companies fail is that they can't hire the right people quickly enough. Use this to your advantage.)

Your goal should be to identify two types of tasks—those that are urgent and important *but lower priority* than others, or urgent

	IMPORTANT	NOT IMPORTANT
URGENT	The potential mentor must do himself or herself now or soon.	The potential mentor can delegate to a mentee or to an assistant.
NOT URGENT	The potential mentor can schedule to do later.	The potential mentor should automate or ignore.

TABLE 2.2 The Urgent/Important Matrix. How busy people prioritize their time.

and not important *but require skills that an assistant may not have.*

Urgent and important tasks usually must be done by the mentor because of his skills and tacit knowledge. Nobody else can do these tasks as well as he can.

For example, if you want to land a mentor who is a popular writer in your niche, urgent and important tasks might look like this:

- Write a new blog post.
- Finish Chapter 3 outline.
- Write a pitch to top three guest blogging outlets.

These tasks require the writer's knowledge in order to do them well. The writer can't (or, shouldn't) give a mentee a blog post to write and then put his own name on it. The writer must write his own writing.

Urgent and not important tasks usually contain a mix of unskilled and skilled tasks to delegate away. Whether or not the potential mentor actually delegates is determined by both his delegation skills and his team.

Unskilled tasks are those that can be handled by an assistant. In the case of the writer example, these might be:

- Send thank you cards to event hosts from last week.

- Schedule next week's phone calls with clients.
- Book travel and living arrangements for next month's conference.

While you *can* offer to take these tasks off a potential mentor's plate, you have to be careful in doing so. You don't want your mentor to see you as an executive assistant. You won't enjoy that work, and it will be a poor fit for both of you.

I once attended a workshop on getting the most out of virtual assistants (VAs). The leader asked the executives attending to describe the issues they had with their VAs. Almost all of the problems came down to variations on one of two main problems:

- Not delegating well
- Not hiring well

In the case of not hiring well, almost everybody who had problems made the mistake of hiring a potential mentee instead of a VA. The people they hired wanted to do what they do now. They didn't want to be professional assistants.

Potential mentees are better to delegate *skilled* tasks to. A VA might know how to schedule calls or book travel for a writer, but she's less likely to know which bloggers to research as potential guest-posters, which publications to target for media outreach, and what kinds of marketing campaigns to run. These tasks don't require advanced skills—but they do require some basic understanding of the writer, his positioning, and the kinds of people who read his content.

The ideal skilled tasks are advanced enough that completing them would be valuable and informative for you but less valuable than other tasks your mentor could do in that time. Your potential mentor has his or her own comparative advantage. Mentors should spend their time on the most valuable tasks based on that comparative advantage.

Identify tasks that they *wish* they had the time to do but simply can't because of other priorities. And then identify what you could *immediately* do that would hook their attention and signal that you're worth their time.

There are three quick ways to do this:

1. **Talk to them.** If you know your potential mentor, ask the person to meet with you and ask her directly what her biggest bottlenecks are. Do not take this route if you don't know the potential mentor, as jumping straight to a meeting or a call is awkward and difficult to do via cold emailing.
2. **Look at their competition and *their* models.** What does their competition do that they don't, but should, and would be relatively easy to do? For example, maybe you want to work with a potential mentor at a small business or a startup. His website doesn't have a lead magnet (a download or gift in exchange for signing up for an email list) but he would benefit from growing his email list. You could develop a lead magnet and recommend a lead capture tool as a way to help grow that list.
3. **Reverse-engineer their goals.** If you know what mentors' goals or incentives are, you can reverse engineer what their likely urgent and not important tasks are. This works particularly well with landing a senior colleague as a mentor because you probably know what the company's goals are and what responsibilities this colleague has. You can also email advisors who do the same work as your potential mentors to find out what kinds of tasks potential mentors need help with.

Make note of what you can create for your potential mentors in your spreadsheet. You can likely reuse the same content or types of content for different mentors, so don't stress too much about being original for each person.

Step 4. Reach Out with a Prepared Value-Add and Be Transparent

Prepare an example of your work that immediately solves a problem for a potential mentor based on Step 3. Reach out directly, be transparent, and let the person know that you want to work with him or her.

You want your outreach email to signal a few important traits:

- **You're not going to waste their time.** The first thought that runs through potential mentors' minds when they get an email from somebody asking to work with them is, "Will this person waste my time? Is it worth it to meet with them?"
- **Humility and curiosity.** Most people who have never worked in a specific role have no idea what goes into it. A potential mentor doesn't want to start working with somebody just for her to leave when she realizes what she actually has to do. Be sincere in your outreach—let them know you don't know much but want to learn more.
- **Digital empathy.** Most potential mentors don't have the time to sit in front of every email for 10 minutes. Make your email compelling and easy to reply to. Put yourself in their shoes by asking, "If I got this email, would I want to reply?"

You can signal most of these traits by sending a compelling email with your value-add attached to it as a "gift." For example, if you reached out to the CMO of a software-as-a-service (SaaS) company whose website didn't have a lead magnet, your email might look like this:

> Hello Dan,
>
> You don't know me, but my name is Stacy Example. I'm an aspiring startup marketer and have followed ExampleCorp for a few months now. Congrats on your recent new round of funding! That must be exciting.

> I'm reaching out because I'd like to talk to you about helping you with your new marketing campaigns. I'm not selling anything—I am just interested in this space and would jump at the opportunity to work with you and your team at ExampleCorp. I've contributed to writing here ***[link]***, here ***[link]***, and here ***[link]*** at various outlets.
>
> I realize you're very busy, but if you'd be open to talking, I can send along a few times we can speak next week. I've prepared a list of responsibilities with which I can immediately help your team.
>
> Is that something that might interest you?
>
> Thank you,
>
> Stacy
>
> PS: I saw you don't have a lead magnet on your site. I went ahead and took your 10 top blog posts and put them into a PDF with a cover from Canva. I saw you're using ConvertKit to collect email addresses. This should work well with their pop-up tools. I've attached the PDF here and recorded a short Loom video here ***[link]*** that walks you through how to install it.. Even if you don't have the bandwidth to speak with me, please feel free to use it. I enjoyed the opportunity to put it together.

This email successfully signals all of the traits that potential mentors would want to look for in somebody reaching out to work with them. The value-add (in this case, the PDF lead magnet) works as a gift that makes the potential mentor think, "This person is probably worth at least talking to." This is true *even if they don't actually need the value-add.*

Your email just needs to be good enough to land a call or a meeting with the potential mentor. Once you do that, focus on going to the call with a list of tasks you can help with. As you talk to the person, be prepared to change the list. The list is, just like the value-add, really just a signaling tool to make the person take you seriously.

Follow these steps and you should be able to land a mentor in as soon as a week. You can use this mentorship to learn and grow a portfolio for your personal brand or even turn it into a dream job offer. Focus on creating immediate and relevant value for busy people and they'll work with you.

When to Move on from Your Mentor

As you improve in your skills, two things happen.

First, you'll develop your own comparative advantage.

Second, since you'll have a comparative advantage, the opportunity cost of your decisions goes up. While it may have once made sense to do menial work, you'll now have higher-value tasks on which you can spend your time.

Don't be afraid to move on from your mentor when this happens. Focus on trading up to a mentor whose time is *even more valuable* and find out what you can do to help that person. Even established CEOs find mentors when they want to take their leadership to the next level.

Simon's Success Story: How to Turn a Creative Hobby into a Paid Career in Less Than Four Months by Landing an Amazing Mentor

Simon (realsimon.com) always knew he enjoyed video production. After he left his job working at a startup, he did some basic freelance work but knew there was more he could do.

Both video production and running a small business require a ton of tacit knowledge to do well. He read books, took classes, and made his own videos, but those left something wanting.

He knew he needed a mentor.

He started by researching a list of all of the video production companies in Charleston, South Carolina. He reached out directly to them through email or Facebook. He told them that he wanted to learn more about how they got started and see if there was a way that he could help. He sent along some of the videos he had already created to show them he wasn't just some charity case looking for free coffee.

He soon landed one reply. They scheduled a time to meet.

While there wasn't immediate work for Simon with the potential mentor he met with, they stayed in touch. This person saw that Simon created videos regularly and wasn't just *talking* about wanting to get into video production. The potential mentor invited him to join his company on a few shoots as a production assistant. These few shoots turned into paid opportunities as Simon proved his competence and took on new responsibilities.

In just a few months, Simon took his hobby to being a paid career with a qualified mentor. We soon started working together when Simon wanted to grow his business and professional network.

KEY TAKEAWAYS

- **Learning from experienced professionals shaves years off your learning curves.**
- **Meet with advisors** to learn from their expertise and experience.
- **Hire teachers** to learn skills and save time that you would otherwise spend self-educating.
- **Land a qualified mentor** by giving a busy professional doing what you want to do reason to work with you.

ACTION ITEMS

1. Who is already in your Cabinet of Models? Who do you already consider advisors, teachers, and mentors? Download the PDF table at zakslayback.com/book/comtable.
2. What kinds of advisors do you need to meet with? Where might you find them? Set a goal to reach out to at least three advisors in the next two weeks. Download email scripts to help you at zakslayback.com/book/scripts.
3. What kinds of skills do you need to learn that you can hire teachers to help you with? Set a goal to set up a consultation call with at least one teacher in the next month.
4. Start the process to land a mentor. Identify a professional goal you want to achieve and make a list of people who have achieved this that you can reach out to. Schedule time to go through the rest of the outreach process over the next two weeks.

CHAPTER 3

Execute

Focus on the Work That Matters, Avoid Burnout, and Feel Confident About Tackling Any New Project

If you want to get something done, ask a busy person.

The Peter Principle is an old idea from management theory. It says that people rise to the level of their incompetence. While this idea is usually used to explain how people need to learn *new* skills after being promoted, it doesn't have to be that complicated to be true. And it doesn't just apply to people in a big corporation.

Most people rise to the level where they can no longer get things done because they burn themselves out doing so much. One of the linchpin skills to succeeding in your career is being able to avoid burnout and continue to get big projects done *as more tasks come your way.*

When you set out to get ahead in your career, you'll blow through your first few Ambition Map Milestones. These are easy-to-accomplish and immediately-available items. You *should* get them done quickly.

But as you pick up mentors, advisors, and teachers, your skills improve and you gain tacit knowledge. Tasks you once found complex and challenging become easy. You become more valuable to your colleagues, clients, employees, or employer. People ask you to do more because they know *you're the person who gets things done.* Combine this with the fact that you now have more skills than you previously did, and it's easy to see why so many people burn out shortly after they make the choice to get ahead.

This makes it ridiculously easy to burn out before you get to the point of establishing a substantive personal brand to make opportunities come to you. You'll want to devote *real* attention to projects that let you show off your skills (you'll use these for your personal brand). You'll want to build *real* relationships with people. And you'll probably want to do more work than you normally would for a while.

You'll want something to help you manage the new projects of hitting your Ambition Map Milestones and learning from your Cabinet of Models. You'll want something to help you avoid burnout.

This chapter gives you that. This is a step-by-step personal project management system designed to help you get done what matters. It's not a life-encompassing productivity system. It's not a big management theory workshop-esque system. It's a system used to help real people generate real results and still manage the rest of their lives.

WHY PRODUCTIVITY SYSTEMS ARE LIKE DIETS

Productivity systems are like diets.

The only things that ultimately matter are that *they get you the results you want* and *you can stick to them.* It also helps if they aren't so unhealthy that they kill you.

If you're thinking, "Oh God, not another productivity system!" don't worry. This isn't a bunch of hodgepodge hacks or a full book on productivity. Instead it's a system to help you manage your own personal projects and confidently take on new work.

Most people approach productivity systems as big life-overhauls. They get to the point of burnout and finally say, "That's it! I need a system!" But when they wait this long, the systems end up failing them for two reasons.

Reason 1: Motivation Schmotivation

The first reason is that productivity systems that overhaul your entire life are hard to stick to. They force big, complicated behavior changes on your life. They're full of flowcharts and complex, expensive courses. But just like that diet that's easy to stick to when you start but slowly falls apart when the reality of life hits you, productivity systems that don't *conform to our existing major habits* fall apart. Quickly.

Overhauling major habits isn't easy. Most people fail when they start big. The entire fitness industry exists on this premise. Gyms fill up after New Year or in the spring in anticipation of Beach Body season and then clear out a few weeks later once the reality of life catches up with New Year resolutions. But most people don't cancel their gym memberships. The many people who fail to go but keep active memberships subsidize the few who go regularly.

When you aren't used to it, going to the gym and taking care of your fitness requires big, unusual habit changes. Canceling subscriptions also falls outside of most people's existing habit patterns. So, gyms stay in business because of people's habit psychology.

This is also why you can't *motivate* yourself to productivity. No matter how motivated you feel to get productive when work gets stressful or you want to embark on a new creative project, motivation doesn't last when it conflicts with existing habits. A bad day, low blood sugar, or a sudden inflow of new work is enough to crush motivation.

Reason 2: Against the Cult of Productivity

The second reason people fall off the productivity system bandwagon is they get too focused on *getting everything done.*

People who get ahead don't get the most things done, they get *the most important things they have to do done.* They're masters of prioritizing what gets results—and actually executing.

The cult of productivity makes people believe that they *must* get as much done as possible. It's what drives people working on their own professional development to focus on the wrong items that make them *feel* productive.

THE RESULT-ORIENT-KEEP (ROK) SYSTEM TO DEFEAT BURNOUT AND TAKE CONTROL OF YOUR SCHEDULE

Stop obsessing over getting everything done.

Start obsessing about *generating results.*

You'll use the ROK system to (1) identify the *Results* that move the needle in your career; (2) *Orient* your schedule so that you get that work done, even when you have other responsibilities; and (3) *Keep* track of new tasks that pop up throughout the day without distracting from the work that matters.

You'll get more important tasks done with this system—without letting your existing responsibilities fall through the cracks.

Most productivity systems fail because they force big, clunky behavioral changes on people and because they don't help you prioritize your work.

The ROK system does the opposite. It's a personal project management system that deals with the realities of a busy life.

Don't Try to Move Mountains Until You Move Pebbles First

The ROK system doesn't challenge you to flip your life on its head and create a ton of big, new habits. Instead, it sidesteps the motivation issue entirely by anchoring Results and Orient planning sessions to your existing *good* habits.

As you read through these pages, ask yourself, "Where are there places in my day and week where I could easily apply this?

What are the habits I currently have around planning and calendaring that I can add this to?"

These existing habits are called *hooks*. Hooks might be having coffee in the morning, brushing your teeth at night, or taking time to do a specific task at work in the morning (even though you don't *need* to do that task). They're habits you *like* and that are pretty ingrained in your life already.

Hook psychology is at the core of the Result and Orient stages of ROK and is based on research from Stanford psychologist BJ Fogg (TinyHabits.com). Fogg has built his career researching how to effectively create new habits and break bad habits. One of the biggest mistakes he's seen people make is trying to create big habit changes out of nothing. Instead, he's found that people develop new habits best when they *anchor* new habits to existing habits. An example he uses is flossing. Most people *know* they should floss, but they don't. Hitting people over the head with the importance of dental hygiene doesn't help. Instead, people only start regularly flossing if they anchor flossing to another existing habit—like brushing their teeth.

Use hooks as ways to make a habit out of the planning steps we're about to walk through.

We also focus on tailoring your schedule to meet you where you are with work. If you benefit from large, uninterrupted blocks of time, you'll schedule more of those for your important work and shuffle your less important work around that. If you benefit from smaller, focused blocks of time, you'll schedule those.

Everything ultimately serves one end: getting you the results that help you succeed.

Result

As your skills improve, you build your brand, and you learn from your models, the last things you'll want to do are busywork, makework, or the *wrong* work that doesn't generate results.

Before your workweek starts, ask yourself what *single result* you need to see *by the end of the week* to get you closer to your goals for the project. This is your *Weekly Result.* Everything else turns on getting this done.

Your Weekly Result is the real, tangible goal that, if you got it done, you could look back at your week and say you did work that *matters.* It's the metric that defines whether or not you were *effective* at getting things done this week.

If you work a traditional job, this could be the assignment or goal given by your manager. If your manager doesn't give specific weekly goals, clarify in your one-on-ones with him or her that your manager wants a *specific* result for the week and focus your attention on generating that result.

If you're self-employed or using ROK to manage projects on the side, use backward induction to break down your quarterly, monthly, or biweekly goals into Weekly Results. Use your Ambition Map Milestones for guidance here.

Let this sentence stem guide you:

> In order to get closer to ***[insert end goal or Ambition Map Milestone]***, this week I must . . .

Your answer should be phrased in terms of *results*, not *tasks.* Focus on outcomes you create and deliverables you generate, not tasks you do. Tasks serve the purpose of generating results. Tasks without results are just busywork. Use active language—avoid "do" and phrases like "wait on," "hope for," or anything else that outsources your agency to other people. The answer to this stem is a result we call the Weekly Result. It's your focus for the week.

Suggested Result Hooks

What positive or enjoyable habits do you already engage in at the end of your weekend and the beginning of your workweek? Do you set your clothing out for work on Sunday night? Do you make sure that you have everything that you have to take to the office the next day? Do you review your calendar to see when you can go out with friends?

Jot down some times in your notebook.

Use these existing routines as hook points for planning out what results you want to generate this week. You can use this same system—identifying existing routines related to the habit you want to develop—to build new habits.

Prioritize to Focus on the Most Important Result

As you finish this sentence completion exercise, you may come up with a few different answers. *Prioritize your answers.* One of the core premises behind the ROK system is that we're bad at properly estimating how much we can get done in a week, so we want to prioritize the most important results that generate the most useful outcomes.

If you could only get one result from the sentence completion exercise done, which would be most useful? Which would open up more doors? Which gets you closer to your end goal?

To make this clearer to yourself, walk through the *outcome* generated by each result and then weigh it against other outcomes.

Every result should generate an *outcome* for you. This might be generating leads; getting information you need; scheduling important, big-ticket meetings; or just finishing a big part of a project. Take every sentence you finished using the sentence stem above and ask yourself, "By generating this result, what do I *get*?" What's the outcome that is generated? Write these down or make mental note of them.

Then take those outcomes and ask yourself, "What can I *do* with this outcome? What doors does this open to help me accomplish my goal?" Which one logically gives you the most information and makes it easier for you to hit your goal?

The result that generates that outcome should be your Weekly Result.

How Do You Define "Important"?

It's easy to get caught up thinking that everything is equally important.

Don't do this.

Everything can be important, but some outcomes are *more important than others*. Usually with any project, you get to bottlenecks in the project. At these bottlenecks, certain specific tasks have to get done to get *more* tasks done. They logically precede the rest of the work.

If you want to host a dinner party, there are plenty of important tasks like inviting people, making food, choosing drinks, choosing dinnerware, and so on. But you can't have a dinner party without *inviting people first.* So, the outcome generated by those you invite logically defines *how much food you need, what kind of food you need, and how to set the table.* The outcome generated by inviting people is the most important of this set because it provides you with the most information and the ability to move forward (Table 3.1).

GOALS	RESULTS	OUTCOMES
Defined by your values and what you or your organization are trying to achieve.	Defined by your goals. Results are the substance behind goals.	The real, tangible information and actions unlocked by achieving results.
Defined in SMART terms.	Defined in outcomes.	Defined in what they'll help you do.
Usually set monthly, quarterly, or annually.	Set at the beginning of your week when you do your planning.	Set when clarifying which results to focus on.

TABLE 3.1 Goals point to results, which generate outcomes. Focus on results that get you closer to your goals.

Example: Jackie's Results

Jackie is an aspiring professional artist and has landed an opportunity to work with a mentor who is a professional artist. The artist has a goal to launch a new studio in town and has brought Jackie on to help her. The studio is set to open at the end of the month, and the artist's goal for Jackie is to help her "create a strong turnout on launch night."

She's defined "strong turnout on launch night" as 80 ticketed attendees. Jackie emailed a local event promoter as an advisor and asked him how many tickets she has to sell in order to get 80 people to show up. He tells her to expect a 50 percent drop-off rate. So now Jackie can rephrase the goal as a SMART goal: "By launch night, I will sell at least 160 tickets for the studio launch."

It's easy for Jackie to just start trying *everything* to get to 160 tickets sold. She can overwhelm herself with Facebook ads, flyers, classified ads, tabling, affiliate deals, and everything else. But this is a recipe for burnout.

Instead of burning herself out, she takes a step back and asks, "What is the *one result* I have to generate *by the end of this week* to set myself up to sell 160 tickets by opening night? I know I'm going to be busy, so I should focus on the most effective use of my time." She comes up with a couple of options through using sentence completion exercises:

> In order to sell 160 tickets by the end of the month, first I have to . . .

She decides on a few options for selling 160 tickets by the end of the month and identifies *one* to pursue this week. That one result she pursues this week is her Weekly Result. If she generates this result this week, it gets her closer to her end goal.

• • •

But, what if Jackie can't decide on which result is the best one to help her sell 160 tickets by the deadline?

She starts by writing down the ideas she came up with to sell tickets:

- Launching a $50 Facebook ad campaign targeted to the artistic neighborhood in town
- Sending an email to the artist's email list asking people to buy tickets
- Handing out 300 flyers at the local university
- Doing customer research by interviewing the 10 people who already bought tickets and asking them what they hope to get out of the event
- Growing the artist's Twitter following so she can promote the event next week

She then breaks down what *outcomes* each of these results would generate for her.

She asks herself, "What will launching a $50 Facebook ad campaign targeted to the artistic neighborhood in town get me?" Her answer is, "I don't know. Maybe some sign-ups?" Her knowledge of her audience and Facebook ads is still so sparse that she can't guarantee any real answers.

Use Your Cabinet of Models!

Sometimes your answer to comparing results *really* is, "I don't know" for every option. If that's the case, reach out to advisors who can guide you.

In Jackie's case, one possible course of action could have been talking to a Facebook ads expert for 20 minutes to get a reasonable estimate on how many tickets she can move with $50 in a week.

She repeats this for every task and realizes that the one that gives her the biggest and clearest result is interviewing existing customers for the event. This lets her know what, exactly, people are looking forward to for the event. *That* lets her know how she should promote it on Facebook or flyers or email campaigns. In other words, that results allows her to drive more powerful results *next* week.

Jackie has identified her Weekly Result to generate.

Result Tools

Since the Result stage is question-based, the best tools for determining your result for the week are writing tools. Don't do this exercise in your head. You should have the result written down somewhere to record and track what you need to do for the week.

- **Notebook.** If you keep a physical notebook or journal and enjoy writing, consider adding a page at the beginning of every week for your Weekly Result. I like paperback Moleskine notebooks (about $10 on Amazon for a set of three).
- **Evernote (evernote.com)** or **Notes (standard on Mac OS).** If you don't like writing by hand, write your results somewhere that is easily accessible so you can reference the result you are working toward throughout the week.
- **Voice Memo (standard on iOS) or Voxer (voxer.com).** If you loathe the idea of writing or paper, a phone, or a computer, you can record yourself asking yourself the sentence stem aloud, and then asking aloud what you get from generating each result.

Orient

Once you have your Weekly Result identified, the primary focus of your workweek should be Orienting your week to generate that result.

Everything else comes second to this.

Don't just find your result and then pull up a to-do list that you think will help you achieve that result. A to-do list–based system will fail you in generating Weekly Results because of two obstacles inherent in to-do lists.

The first is *prioritization of tasks.* Your to-do list may relate to a result, but it is likely just a jumble of items all listed at equal priority. Some get done, some don't. What determines what gets done? Usually expedience, not importance.

Don't let this be the case for you.

The next obstacle is *prioritization of time.* We allow busywork (like meetings and checking email) to suck up time that could be spent working toward generating our Weekly Result. Combine this with the fact that fires and mini-crises pop up during the week and the to-do list doesn't end up getting done and the likelihood of being where you want to be at week's end is low. Assume you'll just barely have enough time in the week and factor in unknown unknowns.

Design your workweek so that it's nearly impossible to *not* make progress on your result. Do this by flipping the workweek script that so many of us learn when it comes to priorities at work.

Avoid Burnout by Orienting Your Week

Too many people's workweeks look like this:

Monday begins with something easy like checking email, catching up on LinkedIn notifications, or writing your to-do list for the week. You tell yourself, "I'm easing into the workday." The first real "work" for the day is a scheduled meeting or call, then you are off to lunch. You come back to start something that is a low priority for a few hours because (1) it's the beginning of the week and you figure you have more time to work on it later; and (2) the carb crash after lunch makes it difficult to focus on anything else. Then you take another meeting or call, spend 30 or 45 minutes on important work tasks, and head home.

Sure, you *did* a lot, but you didn't feel particularly effective. You think to yourself, "It's OK though, I have the rest of the week to focus on getting important items done."

Fast-forward to Friday, and the tasks that drive your result for the week are only half-done. Fires popped up during the week and you misallocated your time. Now you're frantically trying to get the most important tasks done before the end of the week.

At the end of the day on Friday, you close your computer, head home, and are grateful for the weekend. But, you leave feeling burned out.

This story isn't special or surprising. Burnout usually happens because we're bad at predicting how much time we'll have and what may happen in the future. We think we'll have more energy, more time, and fewer tasks later in the week. But the week compounds, and before we know it, we find ourselves under pressure and behind schedule.

So, would you rather *hope* you have enough time in your week to get all your tasks done every week and risk burning out, or would you rather proactively Orient your week to win, no matter what distractions, crises, and carb crashes come your way?

Just like with setting long-term goals, assume that you're bad at predicting the future. Set your schedule so that *even in a worst-case scenario*, you have plenty of time to generate your Weekly Result.

Don't leave your most important, biggest tasks for the end of the week when you're most likely to be burned out and tired.

Here's what this looks like in practice (Figure 3.1).

Schedule the biggest, most important tasks at the beginning of the week and smaller, perfunctory tasks later in the week.

Do this for two reasons.

First, by scheduling your most important tasks earlier in the week, you allow yourself ample wiggle room in case tasks take longer than you expect. Sometimes a task is more complex than expected. Sometimes distractions pop up (we'll talk about how to handle distractions and less-important tasks in "Keep").

Second, by scheduling your most important actions earlier in the week, you have no choice but to start your week tackling the task most likely to convert your week from a null to a win. Plus, the momentum of starting the week off on the right foot will carry

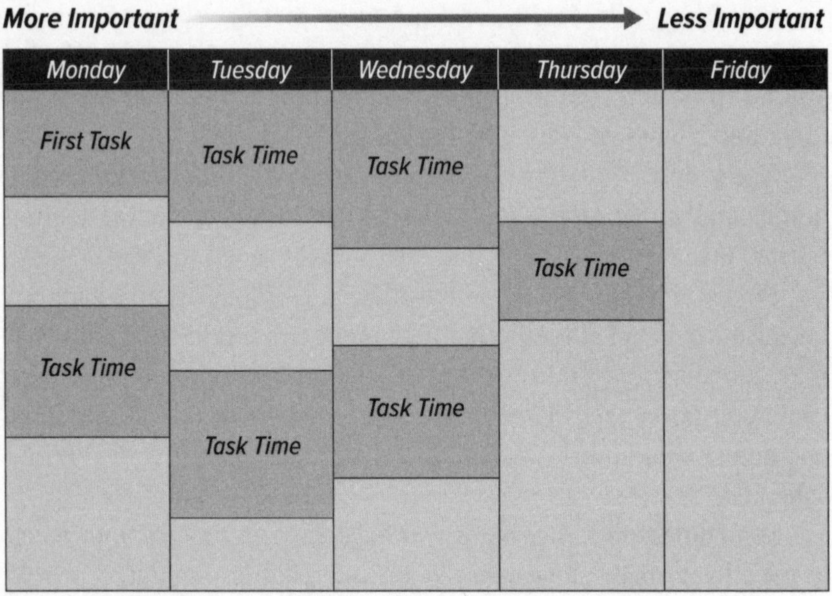

More Important → Less Important

Monday | Tuesday | Wednesday | Thursday | Friday

First Task
Task Time
Task Time
Task Time
Task Time
Task Time
Task Time

FIGURE 3.1 Your most important tasks should come when you're most productive in your day and early in the week. Don't try to "ease into" them and impose task switching penalties on yourself.

through the rest of the week. You'll set up the game to win before you even start playing.

Here's how to do this in practice.

Orient Your Week Using Backward Induction

To figure out what our week should look like, we return to the process of backward induction. You'll ask yourself, "What do I need to do before I can generate my Weekly Result?"

Let's consider Jackie again. Jackie knows she has to interview people who already bought tickets to find out valuable information for her marketing campaign. But what happens *right before* she actually interviews people?

> Before she speaks to them, she has to compile a list of questions.

> Before she compiles a list of questions, she needs to research what questions would be most helpful.
>
> Before she does research on what questions to ask, she needs to get the calls scheduled on the calendar.
>
> Before she gets the calls scheduled on the calendar, she needs to reach out to each of the attendees and ask them to get on the phone with her.
>
> Before she reaches out to the attendees and asks them to get on the phone with her, she needs to craft a compelling email to get a call scheduled.
>
> Before she crafts that email, she needs to pull the list of 10 attendees.

That's it.

Those are all the steps she needs to take in order to generate her Weekly Result. Any further backward induction would be a task-specific item for her, like navigating to the specific portal where she can find the attendees. She has a clear idea of exactly what she needs to do to generate her Weekly Result, and she can start by scheduling "Pull list of attendees," on her calendar for Monday morning.

Follow the same process in breaking down what you need to do to generate your Weekly Result.

Start with a sentence stem:

> Before I ***[insert result you want for the week]***, first I need to . . .

Then, fill in:

> Before I ______, I need to ______.

Continue this process until your answers become task-specific and *immediately* actionable. Your final answer is what I call your First Task.

Find and Set Your First Task

Your *First Task* is the first real work task of your week and should be scheduled for every Monday morning (or whenever you are most effective at the beginning of your workweek). Do not schedule unimportant tasks like "check email" or "browse LinkedIn" before this task.

To put this into practice, first you must confirm that all of your *time-bound tasks* are scheduled for the rest of the week. (Time-bound tasks are those you can't really control when they happen, including meetings, phone calls, or the like that must be completed at a specific time.)

Then, add your First Task into your calendar at the beginning of the week.

If you get nothing else done with your week besides your scheduled items and the First Task, your week should be a net gain.

Schedule Task Times

Hopefully your week is more than meetings and a single task on Monday morning. The rest of your time should be dedicated to generating your result with Task Times.

Task Times are discrete chunks of time that you schedule every day with no particulars in terms of the task at hand, other than getting closer to your Weekly Result. So, rather than plan what exactly you'll do every minute, plan out what topic or result you'll focus on generating during these discrete blocks of time. Give yourself enough time to generate your result while also accounting for the reality that you may fall behind on work or get pulled away during a Task Time.

You may be wondering, "How long do these Task Times need to be?" The answer is, "It depends." The amount of time you mark off in your calendar will vary based on the nature of your work and whether you create a Maker's Schedule or a Manager's Schedule for yourself.

Suggested Orient Hooks

When are you *already* looking at your calendar? Is it Sunday night before you go to bed? Is it at the end of the day Friday?

Write down a few times you already look at your calendar open in your notebook. These will be the ideal times for you to identify and schedule your First Task.

Whenever you have hooks, be sure to Orient your week to the generation of your Weekly Result. All else comes second to that.

Maker's Schedule Versus Manager's Schedule

Paul Graham (paulgraham.com), a Silicon Valley investor and founder of Y Combinator, drew a distinction between two common schedules in his blog post, "Maker's Schedule, Manager's Schedule" (Figure 3.2).

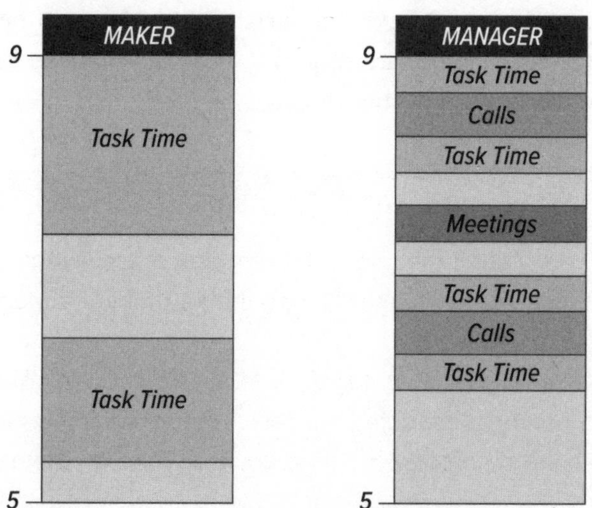

FIGURE 3.2 Maker's Task Times Versus Manager's Task Times

Makers require large chunks of uninterrupted time to generate results. Developers, engineers, designers, writers, producers, and artists commonly fall into this category. Meetings and calls interrupt the ability to create and have considerable negative effects on their ability to create.

Managers require small chunks of time for meetings, phone calls, and delegation-related tasks.

It's possible that you fall into both of these categories, but it's also likely that your tasks *generally* fall into one or the other type of scheduling. With this in mind, be sure to design your days to optimize for that.

If you require Maker time but your day job requires you to follow a Manager's schedule, be sure to schedule a long Task Time that you guard jealously. Remember, once you put your time-bound tasks on your schedule, Task Times are the next chunks of time to be added to your day.

Task Times are *your* time to work on generating your Weekly Result (Figure 3.3).

Any remaining unscheduled parts of your day will be reserved for whatever *Keep* items are required—the distractions and nonurgent tasks that pop up during the day.

The Importance of Timing

Should your Task Times go in the morning or the evening? Before lunch or after lunch? During the workday or before or after work?

That's up to you. How do you work best? If you're not a morning person, schedule your Task Times for the evening. If you are a morning person, schedule Task Time for the early morning.

Workweek with Task Times Example

Monday	Tuesday	Wednesday	Thursday	Friday
First Task	Task Time	Call	Meeting	Task Time
Meeting	Task Time	Meeting	Task Time	Call
Call	Lunch	Call	Lunch Meeting	Lunch
Task Time	Task Time	Call	Task Time	
Lunch	Call	Task Time	Call	
Call		Lunch		
Call		Task Time		
Task Time		Meeting		
		Task Time		

FIGURE 3.3 An example of the ROK system applied to a calendar for somebody who has to do both long periods of uninterrupted work and manage phone calls and meetings. Notice how he has more Task Times at the beginning of the week and fewer at the end—he's preparing himself to get his Weekly Result done early and before any work gets backlogged by the end of the week.

Orient Recap

1. Using **backward induction**, ask yourself, "What do I need to do before I can generate my Weekly Result?" Once you know the answer, break down the steps you'll have to take this week to get to that result.
2. Be sure all of your **time-bound tasks** are scheduled, including meetings, calls, and required tasks outside of your control.
3. Schedule your **First Task**, which is the *very first task you have to take* at the very beginning of your week. Come hell or high water, you'll get this done.
4. Schedule in **Task Times** throughout your week that are conducive to the work you need to do to generate your Weekly Result. The nature of your work—Maker's work or Manager's work—should define the length of the Task Times.

Keep

Distractions happen.

Instead of struggling fruitlessly to eliminate them entirely from your life, detoxing completely from social media, or getting frustrated with others when they ask you to do something, set up a system to *manage* them before they become a problem.

Think about the last time you got immersed in work you enjoyed. Maybe it was writing a blog post or an article, or taking a call or a meeting. After an initial warm-up period, you plow through the work. Then a notification pops up.

Ugh.

This is what is called a *task-based distraction*. These distractions happen all the time: a colleague asks for the latest version of a document, a new email pops up that requires your response, or a client calls with a problem. You think to yourself, "Looks simple enough. This should only take a few minutes." So you handle the distraction and head back to your work. But by the time you handle this distraction (5 mins), let the other party know it's done (5 mins), and get back into the flow of your work (10 mins), your "5-minute" task just devoured 20 or 30 minutes!

Task-based distractions slowly chip away at your scheduled Task Times and destroy your focus. Deal with them later.

Few distractions are truly urgent. Most can wait until you're done with your Task Time.

Keep task-based distractions in a central place that you can access without breaking your flow from the Task Time. In essence, keep a list of "important, but not urgent" tasks as they come in.

As soon as you're done with your Task Time, look at the list you created and address as needed. For example, use the 10 minutes between your Task Time and your call to respond to emails. Use the 23 minutes between a Task Time and lunch to send documents to your client, and spend 5 minutes checking your text messages in between meetings.

Keep distractions separate from Task Times, and you'll find your Task Times more enjoyable and productive.

Keep Tools

The tool you use to keep track of task-based distractions as they pop up during your Time Task is important. Look for an option that minimizes cognitive taxes and keeps you in a state of flow while working. This means choosing a tool you can quickly access without distracting yourself from your Task Time. Product designers call this *low-friction*. If you have to change windows more than once or get up from your chair, it's too high-friction. Choose whatever tool is least distracting for you based on the type of work you do.

Here are some low-friction tools I recommend:

Keep (keep.google.com). Use Google Keep if you live in Gmail, Google Drive, or Google Calendar. You can access Keep directly from each of these and tag documents and emails with tasks, all without changing windows or apps.

Evernote (evernote.com). If you like Evernote, keep this open in a separate window behind the primary task window. Alternatively, you can use the native Notes app on Mac OSX or iOS.

Notion (notion.so). If you need a full-stack tool you can integrate with Slack and use with a team, Notion is hard to beat.

Trello (trello.com). Use Trello if you like the idea of sticky notes or index cards but you want to stay on your computer.

Sticky notes or index cards. When a task-based distraction comes in, just jot it down on a note near you and put it in a pile to attack when you finish your Task Time.

KEY TAKEAWAYS

- **Don't get bogged down in productivity apps, hacks, and tricks.** Most of the time, you don't need to do more—you just need to focus in on the work that generates results.
- **With any project or type of work you're working on, what results move the needle?** How do you get to those results? Don't do work just to feel busy—ask yourself what you really need to do to get the results you need.
- **Before your week starts, schedule in devoted Task Times during the week to generate the results you need.** If you benefit from long periods of focused work, schedule those in. If you benefit from short bursts of work, schedule those in.
- **Guard your Task Times jealously.** Seemingly small distractions quickly turn from 5 minutes into 20 minutes. Set up a low-friction system for keeping distractions to deal with them later.

ACTION ITEMS

Need help implementing ROK? Looking for examples? Visit zakslayback.com/book/rok for a guide to getting started, detailed success stories, and links to all of the tools referenced in this chapter.

1. What kinds of Weekly Results do you need to generate in your work? If you're looking to get a promotion, what kinds of results would make your managers happy? If you're self-employed, what kinds of results move the needle for you?
2. Find a *hook* during your week where you can sit down and plan out the results you need to generate over the next few weeks.
3. Before leaving this hook, ask yourself what times you need to schedule in *this week* to get closer to those results. How long are those times? When do they happen?
4. If you don't already use a master calendar that captures both your work and your personal schedules, start doing so. Avoid double-booking your Task Times. Recommended tool: Google Calendar.
5. Set yourself up on a Keep tool that integrates well with your Task Times. If using an app, I recommend setting it to open on startup (you can do this in your Preferences or Control Panel).

CHAPTER

4

Signal

Unleash a Personal Brand that Grows Your Network, Brings You Opportunities, and Makes the Right People Want to Work with You

A Note to You, the Reader

I want you know that this chapter is *long*. The first half teaches you how to set up your personal brand online. The second half teaches you how to build it out. If you already have a personal website, I recommend skimming the headers of the first half to see if something sticks out to you personally and then diving into the second half. If you don't have a personal website, read this chapter beginning-to-middle, build your site, and then return to the second half.

You have a personal brand, whether you like it or not.

You also have a choice about this brand: do you craft your personal brand and make it work for you, or do you allow yourself and your story to be crafted by other people?

A personal brand is a distilled reputation. It's what others think about you when you're not around. And, it's what traits, skills, and experiences people associate with you.

Your personal brand is a powerful tool for getting ahead. It's your home base for showing the world your skills and the value you create, as well as why and how people can work with you.

In business terms, your personal brand is your own personal marketing department. It's what tells others they should take you seriously.

The difference between a cheesy personal brand and a useful personal brand comes down to substance over fluff.

This chapter teaches you how to craft and grow your personal brand so that the *right* people find you and want to work with you. If you already have a personal brand, use this chapter to fine-tune it. If you don't have a personal brand, this chapter walks you through proven step-by-step processes to build one. You'll learn how master branders use their personal brands to land new opportunities and what kinds of content they create to get the right people interested in them.

MISCONCEPTIONS ABOUT PERSONAL BRANDS

A personal brand is *not* being the guy on YouTube standing in front of his cars. You don't have to "put yourself out there" to have a successful personal brand. If you enjoy using YouTube and video platforms to help others discover you and how you can help them, great. Use them. If not, don't worry. You can create a personal brand without feeling sleazy. It's less about self-promotion and more about signaling positive professional characteristics about yourself so that you can help others who need your skills, experience, and background.

At the same time, it's *not* simply having a blog. A blog plays a role in crafting a powerful personal brand, but a blog alone doesn't do justice to what you know, how you know it, and what value you can create.

It is *not* necessarily running a business as your name. Some people choose to run businesses through their personal brands. That's fine. But you don't have to run a business through your personal brand to benefit from the personal brand that exists without the LLC attached to it.

Think of your personal brand more like a résumé that always works for you, even while you sleep. It helps people you want to eventually work for find you and say, "Yes! This is the kind of person I want to work with!" And, it helps provide a safety net for your career should you decide to leave your job.

And it is *not* just about pursuing vanity.

You can't have a personal brand until you've achieved, built, or overcome *something*. There's a reason this chapter is in the second half of this book. The person who focuses on personal branding before accomplishing anything and creating value looks goofy and projects a negative signal into the world. He projects that he cares more about vanity metrics than about what really matters.

What you achieve doesn't have to be earth-shattering. You don't have to summit Everest while working as a single mother. You don't have to sell a company by the time you're 15. Instead, you just have to own *something* that sets you apart from the average person in your peer group.

A successful personal brand doesn't necessarily attract the *most* people. A successful personal brand attracts the *right* people. This means your personal brand should attract, hook, and keep the attention of people who can give you opportunities. This could be people you can work with, people who can hire you, people you can learn from, or just interesting people you want to meet.

IT'S ALL ABOUT SIGNALING

Everything you do, build, say, and become projects a signal into the world. These signals work as shorthand to help others make decisions like whether or not they should work with you.

Positive signals work like green lights at an intersection, signaling, "It's all right to go, you won't get T-boned by a semi." Negative signals work like red lights, saying, "If you go right now, there's a very good chance you're going to wish you hadn't."

Positive signals show that you're trustworthy, hardworking, and somebody that others want to work with (Figure 4.1). Negative signals show that you're a flake, lazy, and not somebody that others want to work with.

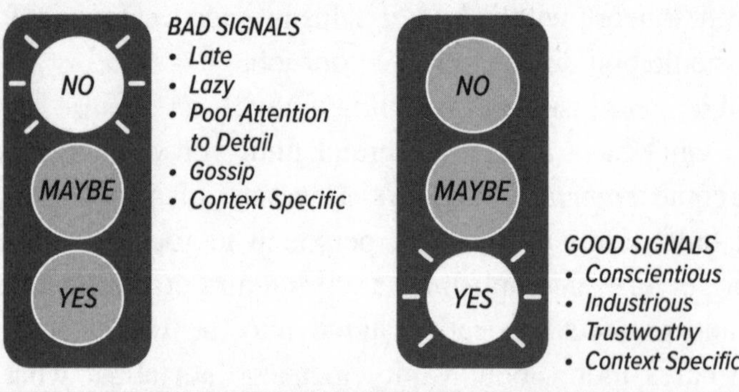

FIGURE 4.1 Everything you do sends a signal about whether or not somebody should work with you.

Two obvious signals that people look for in working with others are work history (where, how long, what role, etc.) and education history (where, how long, what major, etc.).

Somebody who spends years working at a large, competitive firm and rises through the ranks *must* possess certain characteristics to get there. If you meet somebody who is a senior vice president at Goldman Sachs or Google, you instantly make assumptions about the person's personality, work ethic, and values. It's fair to think that this person is conscientious, hardworking, competitive, economically motivated, and moderately conformist (which is not *necessarily* a bad trait).

Somebody who enrolls in Harvard signals certain characteristics, too. Same goes for somebody who chooses not to go to college but rather work on growing her own business.

People make these decisions about you in a split second. Whether or not this is fair is irrelevant—it's simply just a fact of life.

Whether something is a *positive signal* or a *negative signal* is defined by context. Whom are you trying to work with, and *what kind of person* are *they* trying to work with?

Conformity is a good example here.

Signaling for conformity is a *positive* signal in a lot of organizations. Boards of directors and HR departments want executives and employees who will stay within the lines and are reasonably predictable. Selecting for conformity keeps turnover rates low and surprises rare. Despite corporate doublespeak about wanting to work with nonconformists, most organizations like conformists because they align their own interests with that of the company and established industry norms. You don't want an airline pilot who is a nonconformist.

Other people and organizations select for nonconformists. They value what a nonconformist brings to the table more than they value stability and predictability. Some venture capital firms search for companies led by nonconformists for this reason.

What matters *to you* is that you signal the appropriate traits for what you want to achieve. If you want to be a leading therapist, you might not want to signal how disagreeable you are. But if you want to be a successful negotiator, signaling low agreeableness might be a smart strategic move.

Context matters. Figure out what traits you should signal and actively cultivate those in your personal brand.

This is one of the reasons why your Cabinet of Models and your Ambition Map matter. Where you want to go determines how you want to craft your personal brand.

Here are common signaling tools that people use to make decisions about others:

- Credentials
- Work experience
- References and endorsements
- Credibility markers (have you been published or featured in some kind of credible outlet?)
- Portfolio/work examples
- How you dress
- How you speak

Ask yourself, "What *kind of person* do I need to be to achieve what I want to achieve?" This is what you want to signal.

THE PERSONAL BRAND: YOUR SIGNALING HOME BASE

Most people go through their careers passively accruing signals. If they're on the job market, they might load these up onto a résumé or a LinkedIn profile, not really aware of what they're doing. They just know they need to put "good stuff" on their résumé. They hope that this gets in front of the right person and that they are this right person's *right person*.

This is a weak way to go through your career.

Instead of taking this passive approach and *hoping* you signal the right traits and *hoping* the right person sees them, take an active approach.

Collect and cultivate *positive* signals. Put them where the *right* people—future bosses, colleagues, investors, editors, clients—can find them. Make it so that when they find them, they say, "Yes! This is *exactly* the kind of person I want to talk to."

Even better, make it so that the people who *know them* mention you and refer them to you. "Oh, you're looking for somebody who can do that? I know somebody. Here's her website and email address."

Instead of waiting for somebody to stumble upon your LinkedIn profile or get to your résumé at the bottom of a stack of almost-identical résumés, make them come to you.

That's what your personal brand does.

Exercise: Personal Brand Audit

When people reach out to you for the first time and you've never heard of them before, what do you do? What about if you see an article or an interview with somebody and you want to learn more about that person? What if a friend says, "Oh, you should talk to this person"?

You probably google them.

Google is the world's most powerful signaling machine. The signals that once appeared only through credentials or a carefully tailored résumé now appear on the first page of Google.

What do others find when they search your name? What will they think when they search your name?

Do a personal brand audit now. Follow these steps:

1. Open up your browser.
2. Open a private window. Do this because Google tailors search results based on your history.
3. Type your name into the search bar. If you have a common name like "John Smith," then search your name with your city or job (e.g., "John Smith Cincinnati").

What results come up? If important people you wanted to work with were searching your name, how would they feel based on what they saw? Would they think, "Huh, nothing interesting," "*Wow,* this is awful," or "Wow! This is exactly the kind of person I want to talk to!"?

Unless you already have a personal website that you've actively cultivated, your first results should be social media like Facebook, LinkedIn, or Twitter. Your next results might be professional pages (such as a page on your company website), blogs, news, and articles that feature you.

This is what people discover when they look for you. This search should say *something* about you. *You control this.* You control whether a search for your name is remarkable or unremarkable. You control whether or not it leaves an impression on the searcher. And you control whether or not the searcher feels compelled to bring an opportunity to you.

By the time you implement the Action Items in this chapter, you'll know exactly what to put online to take control of your personal brand.

The rest of this chapter shows you exactly how to build a powerful personal brand that brings opportunities to you. This takes some work at first. But the content you'll create and the foundation you'll set are what marketers call *evergreen*, meaning they drive engagement and interest for months and years after created. They work for you while you sleep. You do some extra work up front so you don't have to do more work down the line.

Let's get started.

CRAFTING, POSITIONING, AND UNLEASHING YOUR PERSONAL BRAND

Your personal brand lets you reach anybody in the world at the stroke of a few keys. A mature, powerful personal brand establishes you as a leader in your field. It shows others why they should want to work with you.

Know Your Niche

Focus on getting in front of the right people, not the most people. A personal brand that attracts and retains the attention of the few people who need and want your help pays better than a personal brand that attracts the attention of a large, unfocused group of people. You should have an idea of what "the right people" look like based on your Ambition Map and your Cabinet of Models.

Focusing on the right people not only helps save your time and sanity by keeping you from comparing yourself to others, but it also helps you further signal your strengths through a phenomenon called *local star power.*

When you signal your knowledge, skills, and positive traits *within your field*, you gain a type of status called *local star power.* When somebody has local star power, they assume a higher status to an "in" group of people who know why that status matters.

Think of an artist who is adored for her work among her peers but mostly unknown outside of the art world, or an executive who is respected among investors for turning around failing enterprises but mostly unknown outside of the business world, or a scholar whose work attracts groupies in her own subfield but is largely considered niche and obscure to the outside observer. Each has local star power. If the business executive were to become an artist, he would lose that star power and become yet another starving artist.

Capture local star power by *focusing on the strengths your niche cares about.*

Once captured, local star power lets you quickly become a go-to option for consulting, speaking engagements, and writing opportunities within your niche. You don't need to be the smartest, most experienced, or most talented person in your field. You just need to be good enough compared to the rest so that others take notice.

Don't worry about boxing yourself in. It's better to focus on too small a niche first and then grow than to focus on too big a niche and then shrink.

Your Website

Your personal brand lives on your personal website.

Social media dominates most people's conceptions of what a "personal brand" looks like, but in reality these sites are optimized to drive attention toward advertisers, not you or your strengths. So, use social media effectively: as a tool to drive traffic toward your personal site. If you can't use it for that, don't devote too much time cultivating a personal brand on social media. Don't obsess over Twitter followers or Facebook friends until you have something to show for it and a website to which you can drive them.

Your personal website is entirely owned and operated by you. It's your real estate on the Internet. Here, *you* determine what you want visitors to do on your personal site, how you want them to spend their time, and what message you want them to take from the site.

Most people don't get as much out of their personal sites as they can. They use them merely as a blog and an About page. Think of your personal site more like a company website than a blog.

When you visit a company website, the company has two objectives:

1. Make you take a *specific* action (e.g., schedule a call, download a guide, purchase a product, place an order)
2. Make you leave with a *specific* impression of the company (e.g., "this is a luxury product," "this is a no-BS company," "these people are experts")

You rarely remember company websites that don't achieve both of those.

Your personal website should be no different. You want visitors to take a specific action, and you want them to leave with a specific impression of you and your expertise.

This makes sense when you think about the way somebody finds your website. They find it either through searching your name or through referral—meaning they're *actively searching to learn more about you or the content you create.*

Visitors *want* you to make them take action. They *want* you to leave them with a specific impression. Respect their time by giving them what they're looking for.

Recommended tools: WordPress (wordpress.org) framework hosted on Flywheel (getflywheel.com). Flywheel is a little pricey for hosting but provides direct support should you run into any issues. WordPress is more complicated than other options like Squarespace but is open-source. This means you aren't dependent on a specific company staying in business and you have access to a large and growing library of themes and plug-ins. Your personal website doesn't have to be fancy at first. It should take no more than an hour to get set up on WordPress.

GETTING STARTED WITH YOUR ONLINE PRESENCE

When creating your personal site, there are a few things you must have and do. Without these elements, people either won't find your site or they won't achieve the two objectives above (take a specific action or leave with a specific impression). Follow these steps and you'll have a strong signaling foundation for *the right people* to find you, want to work with you, and have a way of getting in touch with you. This works as your collateral for getting ahead, building your network, and closing new opportunities.

Step 1: Find and Purchase the Appropriate Domain

In most cases, you want your domain to be FirstNameLastName .com. (e.g., ZakSlayback.com).

This makes it easy for people to remember, easy for you to give out, and easy to rank toward the top of Google searches when searching your name. If you can't purchase FirstNameLastName.com, consider FirstNameMiddleInitialLastName.com or FirstNameLast Name.co.

Always own your name domain. The last thing you want is somebody else with the same name taking it or somebody taking it for malicious purposes.

Also consider buying variations on your name and redirecting them to your personal site (e.g., ZachSlayback.com, ZackSlayback .com). You want to make finding you as easy as possible.

Recommended tool: namecheap.com.

Step 2: Create and Put Your Positioning Statement on Your Home Page

Who are you, what do you do, and who do you do that with or for?

That's the question people ask when they land on your site. Immediately answer it for them.

Do this with a positioning statement.

A positioning statement says exactly who you are, what you do, how you do it, and for whom you do it. It doesn't focus on buzz-words or in-the-clouds language like mission statements do. It isn't philosophically charged like a values statement.

If you want to tell visitors more about your values, your mission, or your story, you can do that through your About page and your content. Do not do that up front. If you do not answer the questions at the front of a visitor's mind, most will bounce from your site before they even get to your About page or your blog. You have only a few seconds to answer these questions.

An effective positioning statement makes the right people say, "Yes! This is *exactly* the kind of person I want to talk to."

It also makes the *wrong* people say, "No thanks, not interested."

Strong brands use disqualification as a major component in their positioning. Consider women's lingerie retailer Victoria's Secret.

Having too many nonbuyers meander around a retail store presents a problem to retailers. They have limited floor staff who must pay attention to likely buyers. Men browsing Victoria's Secret because they're bored distract staff from likely buyers (women and men buying for women). So, the store brands itself in strong, audacious feminine colors. This not only attracts the right buyers (women who like lingerie), but also repels nonbuyers.

Or consider Home Depot and Lowe's. Both are home improvement stores, but each is positioned toward a different market. Home Depot, with its bold, construction-like branding and strong colors, is positioned toward contractors (who tend to be men). Lowe's, with its subtle blue and home-oriented branding, is positioned toward women and people renovating their own homes.

You can use the same tactic to focus on what works for your right people.

Before writing a personal positioning statement, ask yourself, "Who do I *not* want to appeal to?"

In my own work, I position myself as a career expert who helps ambitious professionals get ahead in their careers by learning skills school never taught them, like networking, sales, negotiating, and personal branding. By focusing on "ambitious professionals" I disqualify people who are not professionals and people who do not consider themselves ambitious. Does this mean that I *never* work with people who aren't professionals? No. But it allows me to speak to specific problems in specific verticals. If I were to try to appeal to all professionals, my content (and therefore my personal brand) would be so unfocused that it'd be unhelpful.

Remember, you can always *change* your positioning and appeal to larger audiences. But you want to start with small, focused positioning to attract the attention of the right people.

Here's a formula you can use to write your own positioning statement:

> I help ***[target niche] [what you do]*** by ***[process by which you do it]***.

For example:

> I help ***high-growth B2B SaaS startups exceed their sales goals*** by ***building out proven referral systems***.

This positioning statement tells visitors, "If you're interested in B2B sales for high-growth startups, you've come to the right place. If not, thanks for visiting but you probably won't get as much out of this site."

You can take the positioning statement to the next level by using comparison:

> I help ***[target niche] [what you do]*** by ***[process by which you do it]***, unlike ***[common supplier or competitor]*** who/which ***[what they do that is ineffective]***.

For example:

> I help ***aspiring software developers learn how to code*** by ***publishing teardowns of real-world projects, unlike coding bootcamps***, which ***don't walk you through real projects***.

This sets the author apart in the crowded space of software development education. Even better, it sets her apart by telling readers that she focuses on real-world projects and acknowledges that coding bootcamps aren't all that helpful. This appeals to a *specific type of person* that she can then speak to on her site.

At the very least, your site should say who you are, what you do (in terms of the value you create), and for whom you do it.

Step 3: Gather and Share Endorsements on Your Home Page

Collect endorsements from people whose opinions *others* value and display those prominently on your home page.

Endorsements are powerful signaling tools that *show* your visitors that respectable people take you seriously. This brings *social proof.* People often outsource their judgment about others to people they respect or who look respectable. If you're respected and praised by respectable and praiseworthy people, then others are more likely to take you seriously.

You can't just get endorsements from close friends and family. *Of course* your mom and wife think you work hard and always do your best (I hope so, at least).

You want endorsements from people your *target audience* respects and finds praiseworthy. If you can't get industry leaders and well-known people to give you endorsements, your next best option is to collect endorsements from *the types of people in your target audience* and *the types of people they respect.*

You want a visitor to see an endorsement on your site and think, "Well, if he takes her seriously, then I should, too!" They do this when they see people they respect and when they see people *like them.*

As your personal brand grows and more opportunities come your way, you can expand your endorsements to their own page and include as many examples as you'd like.

When you're just getting started, aim for at least four endorsements. You already have a network you can tap for these: your colleagues and your Cabinet of Models.

One of the reasons we build a Cabinet of Models is to build the rapport and experience with respectable and praiseworthy people.

Here's an email script you can use to request an endorsement from people you've worked with, like your Cabinet of Models:

> Hi ***[First Name]***,
>
> I wanted to shoot you an email making a quick request. I've been building out my personal website and am looking to collect testimonials and endorsements from people I've worked with.
>
> I've enjoyed working with you on ***[whatever you work together on; if your mentor, this should be the work you do with them; if your teachers/consultants/coaches, this should be what they teach you; if your advisor, this should be what you two mostly talk about]***. Would you be open to providing a short endorsement for my site? I will include this on the site.
>
> If so, I can pass along a few questions to make it easy and quick for you.
>
> Thanks,
>
> ***[Your name]***

Once they send you a positive reply, you can reply with a message like this one:

> Hi ***[First name]***,
>
> Perfect. Thank you.
>
> Here are the questions I mentioned:
>
> 1. What hesitation or concern did you have before we started working together that would have prevented you from working with me?
> 2. Why did you decide to work with me?
> 3. What results did you see as a product of working with me?
> 4. Would you recommend working with me to somebody you cared about?
> 5. Anything else you'd like to add?*
>
> Thank you!
>
> ***[Your name]***

This makes it easy and quick for people to give details on why they work with you and if they recommend that others do the same. This makes for quality endorsements. A quality endorsement looks sincere, honest, and like it was written by a real person, not a marketing robot.

That's one of the reasons why we ask the first question about hesitations or concerns. If somebody you work with had a hesitation or concern about working with you, chances are a site visitor may, too. Play to your strengths, but don't hide potential shortcomings. Counter them before others can bring them up.

---

* These questions are based on "Six Questions to Get Outstanding Testimonials," Psychotactics, www.psychotactics.com/six-questions-testimonials/.

For example, if you're unusually old or young for what you do, make sure to collect an endorsement from somebody who admits he was at first skeptical due to your age. Preempt objections before they happen.

• • •

Take the answers to these five questions and tailor them into a single endorsement text. Display this on your home page along with the following information about the person who gave the endorsement (Figure 4.2):

- *Full* name (there's nothing shadier looking than endorsements that are just first names).
- Title
- Photo

Optional information that you can include:

- Age
- Location (city and state/province)
- Relationship to you (e.g., client, colleague)

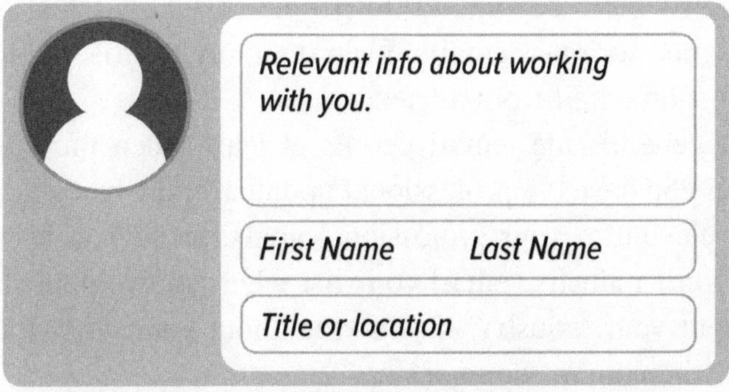

FIGURE 4.2 Great endorsements have a photo, a detailed recap of working with you, and the full name of the person who worked with you. Optional information includes age, title, and location.

Step 4: Create an Email Capture on Your Home Page

Once you've told visitors what you do, for whom, and why they should take you seriously, you want to ask them for their email addresses with an email capture. Do this so that you have a direct line to the right people. Few professional tools are better than a list of people who have actively told you they want to stay updated about your life and work.

Your email capture tells visitors exactly what they get for giving you their email address. Direct updates from you and information about your niche are fine at first. This isn't enough to grow a large email list, but it is enough to get a few people who are intimately interested in you and what you're doing. (See "Lead Magnets" below for advanced content to take your lead capture to the next level.)

Share new content with your email list as you create it. Remember, these are people who have *chosen* to give you their email addresses. They are personally interested in what you have to say and your work. Reach out to them regularly and update them.

Don't worry about making your email updates look like flashy newsletters. Write your email updates as if you were writing to a friend or a colleague. For years, I composed all of my emails in Gmail as plain text and just BCC'd my entire email list. It wasn't until my list grew beyond 1,000 people that I switched to a service designed for mass emails. Even then, my emails still look like they're just an email from a friend.

As a general rule, email people at least when they join your list, when you have big professional updates, and when you produce content relevant to your professional goals. So, if you write about news in your industry, email your list when you've published new posts about your industry. If you vlog about your daily life, email your list when a new vlog goes up.

Here's an email script you can use in your welcome message:

Hey there,

Congrats on joining my email list. You'll receive updates directly from me about ***[your specific niche]***.

I'm curious—what made you join my list? Can you tell me a little about yourself?

I read every reply. Looking forward to hearing from you.

[Your name]

For this to work, you *do* have to read every reply.* Don't expect everybody to reply—but pay attention to who does. Those people instantly qualify themselves as particularly interested in your personal brand.

Directly asking your audience why they decided to join your list lets you know what messaging works. Double down on that messaging to learn more about your audience.

You may discover you have experienced and established professionals in your field joining your list. These could be future bosses, collaborators, clients, or business partners.

Recommended tools: mailchimp.com. While WordPress does have its own native email capture to update subscribers when you make new posts, it sucks. Mailchimp provides an affordable (free for fewer than 3,000 subscribers) option to capture and contact visitors. Alternatively, you can use ConvertKit (convertkit.com).

Step 5: Create Your About Page

You've told visitors who you are, what you do, and why they should take you seriously. You've captured contact info for them. Now they want to learn more, and they will visit your About page to do this.

* This is a marketing strategy I call "Conversational Conversions." Read more on it at zakslayback.com/conversational-conversions.

Most About pages are awful.

They're either the author's biography or full of corporate doublespeak jargon (no, you probably aren't actually "passionate about utilizing synergy among teams").

Your visitors don't care that much about you. They don't care about jargon and buzzwords. They care about what you can do for them.

An excellent About page is about your audience. It walks them through the value you create for them, how you create that value, and speaks to the problems already in their minds. For a company brand, this means speaking to customers' problems on an emotional and visceral level. It means identifying their problems, identifying what those problems feel like, and describing how the company solves those problems.

For a personal brand, this means speaking to what your visitors like most about your story, content, or material. Identify the issue or reason most people visit and enjoy your content, tell your story (to the extent that it illustrates how you can help them), and ask them to join you (add an email capture to the bottom of the page).

If you need a biography on your site, *link to it* on your About page. For example, if you speak at events often, insert a link at the bottom of your page labeled "Event Bio."

Let's take a look at two introductory paragraphs for the same person's About page:

1. Sarah is a journalist writing about issues of technology, democracy, and ethics. She received her BA in philosophy from Columbia University and interned with Ezekiel Emanuel in the Obama White House. . . .

or

2. Have you ever wondered how to make sense of daily news about tech and democracy? It feels like every day there's a new story about the implications of a clash between these forces. Will technology save democracy?

> Or will it be its downfall? My name is Sarah, and I write on these issues. After spending years working with the country's leading bioethicist, I've developed an obsession with making sense of the intersection of technology, democracy, and ethics. . . .

Which one makes you want to join that person's email list?

The second one.

An advanced tip my teachers taught me is to use *the exact language* your visitors use to describe their own experience in your niche (yet another reason you want to email people when they join your list). And avoid marketing jargon. Real people don't say "synergy" and "collaboration." Use language real people use.

Include another email capture at the bottom of your About page. A well-written About page *compels* the reader to ask, "OK, you've read my mind. I'm ready. What do you want from me?" Make it easy for them and give them the answer right on that page.

Step 6: Start Your Blog

The heart of your personal site and personal brand is your blog. Publish content that the right people want to see, read about, and listen to. Answer questions, tell stories, and signal not only your knowledge, but also your ability to communicate.

A personal blog should focus on a web of similar topics. You don't want to write about baking one day, sales the next day, and how much you like cats the day after that (unless selling baked goods to cats is somehow your niche). Readers should be able to tell what kinds of topics you write about from a quick glance at the titles of your blog posts.

Get in the habit of writing and schedule it into your week. Set aside Task Times devoted to writing. Your *initial* goal is *not* to create remarkable, world-class content. It's just to create. Once you get in the habit of writing regularly, *then* you can focus on creating higher quality, longer-form content that appeals directly to your audience. For now, just get started.

Can You Post Too Often?

Probably.

But this is a problem few people face.

Most people never get in the *habit* of creating new content, so they create a few posts, ignore their site, and then create a few more posts months later.

Don't do this.

Focus *first* on building the habit of creating content. *Then* focus on whether or not you should post every day, every other day, or once a week.

One of my early mentors challenged mentees to write every day for a month. By the end of the month, writing new content seemed like no big deal. The point wasn't to create remarkable content. The point was to overcome the barrier most people have to shipping content and create a habit of content creation.

The hardest part about creating content is knowing what to write about. As you grow your email list, ask the list directly what questions they have that you can answer. Answers to this question can become new blog posts, vlogs, or emails.

Here's an email script you can use to send to your list:

> Hey there,
>
> I wanted to shoot you a quick message and ask, what questions do you have about ***[your positioning, e.g., marketing, sales, freelance writing, baking, art]***? What questions can I answer for you?
>
> I'm looking at upping my content creation, and any ideas you have are greatly appreciated.
>
> Thanks!
>
> ***[Your name]***

If you don't have a list or a group of people you can ask for ideas, consider question-and-answer sites like Quora (Quora.com). (Quora also doubles as a "Personal Brand Builder." See the section on this later in this chapter.)

As you create content, you'll discover some topics get more traction and drive more interest than others. Pay attention to this and double down on what works. Focus content creation on content your audience finds helpful and engaging. Professional content creators have tools to track engagement. When getting started,, just listen to your audience. They'll tell you what they like and find helpful. Your content will drive engagement through your funnel (Figure 4.3), driving people to sign up for your list—or making them reengage through your list after they've already signed up.

Your blog also serves as a place for video, audio, and visual content you create. If you prefer vlogging or podcasting to writing,

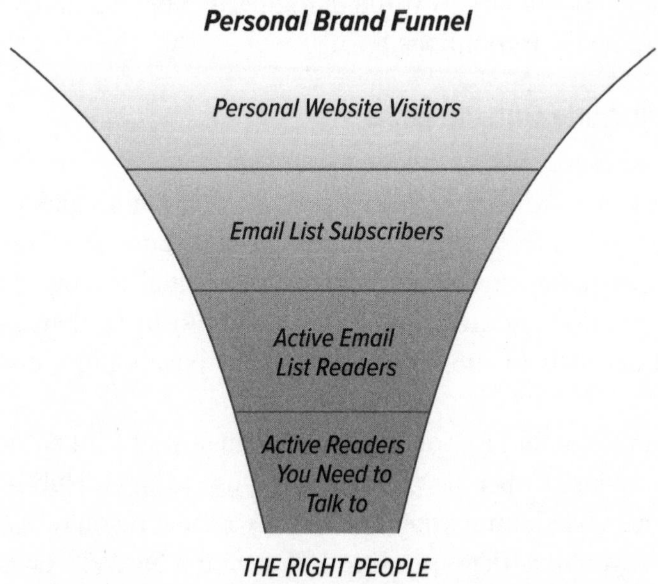

FIGURE 4.3 Your personal brand funnel. After visiting your website, you want *the right people* to join your email list and then engage with it. Your site serves the purpose of attracting, hooking, and keeping *their* attention.

that's fine. Just post your vlogs and podcasts as unique posts on your blog with short write-ups. This drives search traffic to your personal site. Google indexes the content of text posts, not audio and video (as of now).

Here are some ideas for blog post topics when starting out. These types of posts are strong signaling tools. They show you have unique knowledge and skills and a level of conscientiousness above the norm:

- "How to" posts
- Book and movie reviews relevant to your audience
- Success stories of personal and professional projects
- Personal narratives that tie into your positioning (i.e., "How I . . ." posts)
- FAQs about your career
- Documentation of what you're learning
- Current events related to your industry (e.g., Josh Blackman built his brand largely through regularly blogging about Supreme Court opinions.)

Step 7: Include Outside Links

Include relevant outside links on your site.

The key word here is *relevant*. Your positioning and your use of other platforms determines relevance. If you use your Instagram account to share interesting information related to your personal brand, go ahead and link to it. If you use it mostly to share pictures of food and cats (assuming this isn't your positioning), don't link to it.

As a rule of thumb, you'll want to include your LinkedIn profile and any industry-specific platforms you use (e.g., GitHub if you're a developer, Medium if you're a writer, YouTube if you're a vlogger, Vimeo if you're a video producer). If you're a business owner or a partner in a business, link to your business.

Put these on the home page header or footer and/or on the navigation tab.

Step 8: Add Your Contact Info (Not a Form)

The right people need to know how to reach you—make this as easy as possible for them.

Be sure you state clearly that visitors can reply to the emails you send, but also have a contact page where they can directly reach out to you. On it, list your email address and tell people why they may want to reach out to you. Don't use a stock contact form. You're a person, not a government bureaucracy.

Don't worry about putting your personal information out there. Spam filters catch most spam, and you don't have the profile (yet) to worry about getting too many emails. Even once you have a larger profile, you can still build that direct relationship with a well-managed inbox. One of my teachers gets over 1,000,000 visits to his site every month and *still* advertises his email address. You're not too busy to receive a few emails from interested visitors.

ADVANCED ELEMENTS OF A PERSONAL SITE

You now have the basic elements to take control of your personal brand online. After indexing on Google, your site should appear on the first page when people search your name. Point new business acquaintances to your site. Use it as your professional and personal hub online. When I go to events, if people ask for a business card, I just tell them to join my email list at zakslayback.com and I'll follow up with them.

As you grow your personal brand, new qualified traffic lands on your site. What you *don't* want is the new traffic landing on your site, getting the gist of what you do, and then just leaving to never return. You don't want to have to rush to create new content just to keep your visitors engaged. Build a site that markets your skills, knowledge, and competence while you sleep.

To do that, build out some advanced functions on your site and *only build these out once you establish a strong foundation.* I didn't build these elements out for a few years, and a lot of the success stories I've seen and worked with didn't have these when they started. But if you want to really set yourself apart from everybody else with a personal site, these elements take you to the next level. They guarantee engagement with the right people while you're busy creating value, generating results, and getting closer to your goals offline.

Lead Magnet

When was the last time you parted with your email address in exchange for joining a "newsletter" or "daily updates"? Unless you really cared about the subject matter, probably never.

When was the last time you gave your email address to a website in exchange for a guide, a book, a free course, or some kind of tool that directly solves a problem you have? Probably recently.

A lead magnet is exactly that. It's an incentive for your visitors to give you their email addresses, join your email list, and stay engaged with your content. You'll get *some* email subscribers without a lead magnet—probably people *personally* interested in you or who really enjoy your original content. But, you'll get *a lot more* with one. A good lead magnet can increase the conversion rate of site visitors to email subscribers by more than three times.

Lead magnets don't have to be complex to work. They just need to be *good enough* to get people to give you their email addresses.

Choose a lead magnet that is relevant to your positioning, *directly* helpful to some issue or problem already in your visitors' minds, and immediately accessible.

Here are some examples of successful lead magnets:

- Sample chapters from your own books (PDF)
- Checklist guides (PDF)
- Email scripts (PDF)
- Conversation starters (PDF)
- Meal plans (PDF)
- Fitness guides (PDF)
- Recipe books (PDF)

- Free courses relevant to your audience (upload these to udemy .com or host them natively with vimeo.com or wistia.com).
- Exclusive interviews with interesting people (PDF or audio file)
- Success stories of projects or clients you've worked on/ with (PDF)
- Public domain books available at gutenberg.org (PDF or .mobi e-book)

You can always change your lead magnet in the future. For years, my lead magnet was an offer to get free books in the public domain every Friday as part of "Free Book Friday." I chose books directly relevant to career success. Eventually, I developed my own original lead magnets based on talking to my audience and finding out what their biggest pains were.

Just get a lead magnet that is "good enough" to make a qualified visitor want to join your email list.

> **Recommended tool:** Mailchimp and ConvertKit both let you set up lead magnet downloads when people join your email list.

Drip Campaign (or Automated Welcome Emails)

If this all sounds like a lot of work, don't worry. You don't have to think about keeping your email list engaged while also constantly writing new content on top of whatever your day job looks like. You can automate contact with your subscribers by setting up a *drip campaign.*

Once subscribers join your email list, send them emails when you publish new content, have relevant updates, and want to engage them. After this, set up an automated drip campaign.

Automated drip campaigns guarantee that subscribers get new emails from you, even when you're busy working, sleeping, or creating new content. They take the stress out of, "Did I email my list recently?" Email funnels also help you stay front-of-mind for your subscribers. If they don't see you once a week or so, they may forget that they joined your list in the first place. Keep them engaged at first so that they come to look forward to a new email from you.

To build your drip campaign, schedule engaging, high-quality emails to go to new subscribers. You can either create these emails as new content or you can reuse old emails that you sent to your list *before* you set up a drip campaign. If you reuse old emails, make sure to set your drip campaign settings to only send the campaign to new subscribers (so that old subscribers don't get the same email twice).

Good-Enough Standard for Emails

Engaging emails should *at least* have an open rate and click-through-rate above your industry average. You can find your industry average here: mailchimp.com/resources/email-marketing-benchmarks/.

Select *at least five* drip campaign emails. If reusing old emails, remove any references to current events (you want your content to always be relevant). Schedule the first email to send no more than one week after a subscriber joins your list. Schedule the next one to send a week after that, and the next one a week after that, and so on.

Congrats! Now you have an automated drip campaign so that new subscribers continue to get updates, even while you're busy working on other tasks.

Recommended tool: Mailchimp and ConvertKit have great automated campaign functionality.

Portfolio

It's one thing to talk about your work and broadcast endorsements. It's another to lay your work on full display.

If you work in a field building tangible deliverables—whether that's physical products, art, photography, writing, software, pitch decks, or design—you can and should show off a portfolio of your work.

Most Portfolio pages on personal sites are little more than a few pictures or links to previous projects. While better than nothing, this doesn't give context for what the project goals were, what you contributed, how you did that, and what results the project generated.

Remember, the goal of each page on your website is to signal the *right traits* to the *right people*. If you want to signal conscientiousness and creativity, give examples that show you're a conscientious and creative person. If you want to signal agreeableness and an ability to pull disagreeing parties together, give examples that show you're an agreeable person with an ability to pull disagreeing parties together.

Every portfolio example on your site should include these elements:

- Who the project was for
- What the client/business/employer wanted out of the project
- What results you got them
- Any interesting facts about how you did it
- Specific endorsements, testimonials, or feedback from the people you worked with on that project, following the rules of endorsements mentioned above

Résumé Lead Capture

LinkedIn lets you see most of the recent views of your profile. If you're on the job market, have your own business, or do a lot of relationship-building in your work, this feature is worth its weight in gold. You know *exactly* who viewed your profile and when they viewed it.

You can build a similar feature on your own site. If you choose to list your résumé or CV on your site, don't just link to it or paste it into a page. Instead, set up a unique email capture.

Just like with the email capture on your home page, assign a lead magnet to this new email capture for your résumé. The lead magnet for your capture on this page isn't the lead magnet you have on the rest of your site—it's your résumé. In order to see your résumé, visitors must give you their email address and first name. They then get access to your résumé. You can then set up a welcome email that goes out to anybody who downloads your résumé (you can set this email to go out only during business hours to make it look more authentic).

Here's what that email might look like:

> Hi ***[First Name]***,
>
> I just saw you downloaded my résumé on ***[your website URL]***. I wanted to personally reach out and see if you had any questions I can answer.
>
> If you don't mind me asking, what is it that you do?
>
> Thanks,
>
> ***[Your name]***

While most people won't respond to this email and are probably just curious about your résumé, *some will respond*. Those who do will let you know if they are potential employers, clients, business partners, or just interesting people you can talk to. Take the conversation from there.

Recommended tool: Mailchimp or ConvertKit, following the same setup you would use for a lead magnet and a drip campaign.

Credibility Markers

Institutions and publications work for decades establishing credibility. Universities vie for top talent so they can point to the successful as alumni. Publications compete for the next big story or scoop. And it works. Employers, researchers, and parents come to respect some colleges and institutions more than others. Readers respect publications that consistently put out high-quality work.

You don't have to spend decades building up your own credibility. You can take advantage of the credibility *others* spent years building by displaying that *these institutions and publications* consider you credible. Displaying logos of institutions, publications, and companies you've worked at or with, or been published in signals to visitors that you're credible and worth listening to. You typically do not need permission to display publication logos, but you should ask permission of organizations with which you work.

Consider displaying these types of logos on your home page:

- **Publications.** Where have you contributed as a writer? Which publications have written about you and your projects?
- **Universities.** Where have you spoken as a guest lecturer? Where have you worked or researched?
- **Organizations and companies.** Where have you spoken? For whom have you consulted?

As with all signaling, *context matters.* You don't have to display a Harvard or New York Times logo for a credibility marker to work. You want to display markers that *your target audience* recognizes and finds credible.

Don't display markers that your audience won't respect. For example, if your target audience is homeschool moms, don't display a *Playboy* logo on your page even if you've written for them before.

Media Page

As you build your personal brand, you'll appear on podcasts, radio shows, YouTube shows, and possibly even mainstream television. Accelerate the speed at which you get invited on media appearances by including a Media page on your site.

One of my teachers once told me he wishes he had spent more time working on media when starting out. I was surprised to hear this, because he's a guy who focuses a lot on direct marketing like email. "The media reads the media," he told me.

When hosts, podcasters, and producers look for new guests for their shows, they look for social proof from other media.

Embed examples on your Media page. Choose examples that play to your strengths. If you speak well and look good, include YouTube videos. If you're a great speaker but uncomfortable on camera, embed audio files.

Include your email address at the top of the page in a block of text directly telling visitors what you can speak about and how they can contact you about media opportunities.

If you suffer from stage fright or can't communicate verbally, invest in communication courses. Somebody who has 80 percent knowledge on a topic but can speak well lands more opportunities than somebody who has 95 percent knowledge but can't speak.

Only focus on a Media page once you have a clear reason for landing media appearances and after you have at least two or three solid examples of media content. Focusing too much on media too early can be a negative signal that you care more about vanity than substance. As with everything in personal branding, make sure your substance is there *before* you start branding.

Copywriting

You can tell a lot about people simply by the way they write. From the words they use, to their cadence, and even the length of their sentences, you see what kind of person they are. They just *sound* laid-back, or formal, or friendly, or authoritative, or antiestablishment, or like they'll call you on your BS.

This is often intentional.

Master communicators, marketers, and branders study copywriting to make their target audiences feel like they're speaking directly *to them*. They also study it to make people *outside* their target audience *dis*qualify themselves. If you don't enjoy the way somebody writes, you probably won't enjoy working with them.

Compare the style of writing on TheArtOfManliness.com to JamesAltucher.com to TheMiddleFingerProject.org. Even if you removed identifying details about each site (e.g., references to

"Manliness" and men from writing on TheArtOfManliness.com), you could *still* tell which writing belonged to which site based on the style. That's because these content creators know what their audiences like, know how they talk, and know what to speak to. You, too, can do this.

Copywriting isn't a feature or a functionality you build into your site like the others in this section. It's a conscious writing approach to make your audience say, "Yes! This is exactly what I've been looking for." It's what makes some writing "stick" and some writing fall flat.

Unless you're a professional marketer and want to do a deep dive in copywriting, just start by familiarizing yourself with common content styles, talking to your audience, and choosing a style that works well for you. Copywriting is decidedly *not* like technical writing. It should sound like how you would speak.

> **Recommended tool:** Abbey Woodcock is a professional copywriter who writes at onlifeandwriting.com. She has a guide on her site (an example of a lead magnet) that identifies five common copywriting voices. For example, my styles are authoritative, learn-with-me, and a little antiestablishment. This looks like my no-frills, straightforward writing that explains both why and how. You may find something different works for you.

PERSONAL BRAND BUILDERS

You can have the best personal website, the finest positioning, the greatest content, compelling copy, and clear evidence and endorsements of your ability to create value. But that all doesn't matter if you don't get the right people to visit your site.

I've seen far too many bright, hardworking people give up at building out their personal brands after they build their website because they don't immediately see a flood of traffic. If you opened a restaurant and didn't advertise it, you wouldn't expect people to visit. Why would you expect something different for your personal brand?

You have to put in some work to get your personal brand in front of people, just like marketers and advertisers do for corporate brands.

To do this, use *Brand Builders* (Figure 4.4). These drive traffic from where your audience already spends their time online.

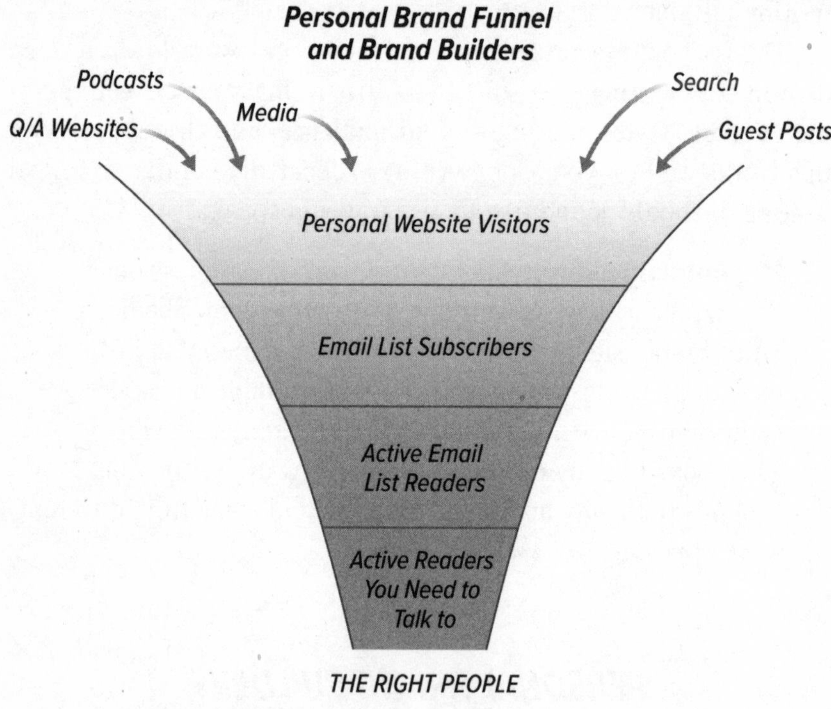

FIGURE 4.4 Brand Builders drive more traffic to the top of your personal brand funnel; they also provide networking opportunities.

The good news is that brand building both pays off for a long time and has a compound effect. Well-crafted Brand Builders are evergreen and allow you to produce larger and larger Brand Builders. An article or feature published five years ago can still drive traffic today.

Real estate developers understand the power of Brand Builders. They strategically choose tenants for shopping centers based on who the other tenants are. If a shopping center has a big Saks Fifth Avenue store, the developers *know* a certain kind of client will come to the center. They'll recruit *smaller* tenants who benefit from the customers already visiting Saks Fifth Avenue. The smaller tenants don't have to fight to get people to come to them—they go where their ideal clients already are.

Imagine reading an article about fitness that answers a question you had in one of your favorite fitness newsletters. In the article, you see the author also has a checklist to help you get the most out of your time at the gym. You click the link for the checklist and end up on the author's site. He used a Brand Builder to get you to join his email list.

When people land on your site through a Brand Builder, offer them a lead magnet *specifically tailored to them based on where they came from.* Understand your audience and understand what unique value proposition you offer them.

1. **Audience.** Place your Brand Builders on platforms, sites, and media that have an audience *relevant to your positioning.* If your positioning targets senior executives at Fortune 500 companies, don't waste your time placing Brand Builders on Thought Catalog and vice.com, which are read by a younger audience. Where does *your* ideal audience spend time online? Go there. Don't know? Interview people in your ideal audience to find out.
2. **Brand Builder lead magnet.** Most people won't just click to your website out of curiosity. They're busy. They have other things to read and do. Give them a *reason* to click. Tailor a lead magnet specifically to them based on why they visit your site. What might work well for one audience doesn't necessarily work well for another, even though both fall into your positioning. Take this into account when pitching new Brand Builders.

Use the following proven Brand Builders to drive traffic and the right people to your site. Some work better for different audiences and for different styles. Some audiences don't read blogs. Others don't listen to podcasts. Others don't use social media to consume content. As you learn more about your audience, double down on where they spend their time. Track which Brand Builders work and which don't for you.

Building and Hosting Brand Builder Lead Magnets

Every time you get featured on another platform, website, or publication, create a landing page on your website with the Brand Builder Lead Magnet tailored specifically to that audience. Link to that landing page in your featured content—even just a link in your bio. Use simple language like, "Welcome ***[other publication name]*** readers/listeners!" and show them exactly what they get for downloading the new lead magnet.

> **Recommended tool:** Mailchimp and ConvertKit have landing page features you can use. I also recommend OptinMonster (optinmonster.com).

Quora/Reddit/Niche Q/A Sites

Some of the most accessible places for Brand Builders are websites that specialize in crowdsourcing questions. Quora.com is the gold standard. Specific subreddits on Reddit, like r/careeradvice and r/personalfinance, also specialize in crowdsourcing answers to questions.

Any user can answer questions posted by other users on these sites. Others then upvote (or downvote) answers based on their quality. In the case of Quora, moderators may select specific answers to feature to the wider platform, either on the home page or through an email newsletter. Quora has a significant audience of contributing editors to other publications—meaning these editors may see an answer and republish it on their own publications (e.g., Thought Catalog and the Huffington Post often repost from Quora).

Cite relevant content on your personal site and encourage readers to keep reading there. Keep self-promotion tasteful and note *why* you're linking to your own site. Most readers don't mind self-promotion so long as it isn't overt advertising.

Learning curve: Low.

Recommended tools: quora.com, reddit.com. Both of these sites have follower and upvote systems, meaning quality answers on well-followed questions can help you capture future readers in the form of followers and upvotes.

Quality of audience: Variable. These sites are better for getting your feet wet writing. If you hit your stride publishing on them, though, double down on it.

Interview *Other* People on Your Site

Take advantage of established audiences by interviewing other people who have their own personal brands. Publish these interviews as blog posts on your site.

Make a list of at least 12 relevant people related to your positioning you can interview. I recommend doing this on a spreadsheet. Organize them into four separate tiers of how hard it would be to get them to say yes. Label these "Easy," "Moderate," "Hard," "Reach." Then add columns for how large you believe their individual audiences to be, their contact info, recent interviews, their own websites, and anyone who can do an introduction for you.

Great interviewees are both *believable* and *have their own audiences*. You want guests who can explain what they know to an intelligent lay audience. You also want guests who have followers who, when the guest shares your interview with them, will read it because they follow that guest (Table 4.1).

	BELIEVABLE	NOT BELIEVABLE
DEVOTED AUDIENCE	Ideal guest. Expert with a niche following.	Charlatan or hack. Associating with these people can damage your brand.
NO AUDIENCE	Interesting character. Interview once you have a following to boost their profiles.	Not interesting. Avoid.

TABLE 4.1 The kinds of guests you want to feature. Feature people who are believable and have a strong following.

Boxed Element: Trading up the Chain

You probably can't land your top-tier blog pitches, interviews, podcasts, shows, or, really, anything when you just start building your brand. Have a top tier in mind but start with smaller, more accessible targets.

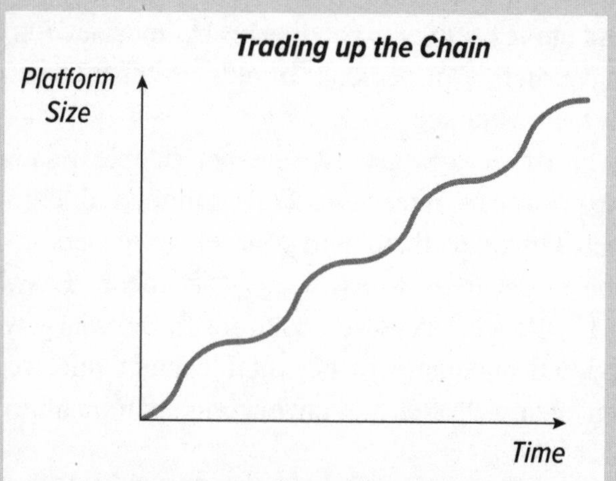

FIGURE 4.5 Trading up the Chain.

> Marketing expert Ryan Holiday calls this *Trading up the Chain* (Figure 4.5). You start with small, accessible targets and then use the fact that they featured you to pitch slightly larger targets. You then use the fact that *they* featured you to pitch even larger targets. Repeat until you get to your top-tier targets.

Choose a topic you'd like to interview guests about based on recent interviews and content on their own websites. This topic should be relevant to your own positioning and interesting enough to their own story that they'd enjoy answering questions about it. Have fun and make it easy for the interviewee to have fun, too.

If you have mutual connections to any of the targets, send these connections an email requesting an introduction. Let them know you want the introduction so that you can do an interview you'd like to feature on your site.

Draft emails to each of the people you chose. You probably won't hear back from your "Reach" and "Hard" targets until you have "Moderate" and "Easy" targets already featured on your site. You can still reach out to them to see what they say. They may say yes.

Here's an email script you can use for a cold email:

> Subject Line: Email Interview Request
>
> Hi ***[First name or title + last name]***,
>
> My name is ***[your name]***. You don't know me, but I am ***[your positioning]***. I'm a follower of your work on ***[specific niche of theirs you know about]***. I particularly enjoy ***[sincere, specific compliment about part of their work]***.
>
> I'd like to interview you on the topic of ***[specific topic]*** for a feature on my site. I think your unique perspective can be really useful to my readers ***[because of a specific reason]***.

> ***[Optional: Mention your audience size and promise to promote the interview to your audience. Skip this if your audience is still fewer than 1,000 subscribers.]***
>
> Is this something you'd be open to? If so, I can send along all the specific questions I'd like to ask you and you can answer at your convenience.
>
> Thank you,
>
> *[Your name]*

This script is easy for recipients to reply to and lets them know exactly what you want. It's respectful because you don't throw all the questions at them until they agree to do the interview. They may say no—that's OK. But most "Easy" and "Moderate" targets find interview requests flattering rather than annoying. For most "Hard" and "Reach" targets, you have to give them a compelling reason to say yes. A large audience or social proof from people *they* respect are often good enough compelling reasons.

Be sure to follow up *quickly* with the questions. Wait no more than 24 hours to send your questions along.

Publish the answers as an interview post on your website. Be sure to include the interviewee's name in the post title (this helps for search traffic, e.g., "Interview: Dr. Jason Brennan on Succeeding in Academia"). Send the interviewee an email when the post is live thanking them for their time and asking them to share the post with their own audiences.

This drives the interviewee's audience to your site and provides evergreen search content related to the interviewee. If people are searching for this person and they find an interview with him or her on your site, they're likely the right people.

Learning curve: Low. The trick is getting the interviewee to share the interview.

Recommended tools: FindThatLead (findthatlead.com) for finding email addresses. Boomerang (boomeranggmail.com) for tracking whether or not recipients open your email and scheduling follow-ups.

Quality of audience: High.

Publish Original Book or Course Reviews

Before most people buy a book, course, or informational product, they look online to read more about it. Detailed, high-quality notes enjoy devoted audiences of high-quality readers. These are people who want to read more books or spend money on courses and want to go into more detail than a simple review offers. Drive this traffic both through search and through sharing the notes with authors and targeted audiences.

For books, this works best for nonfiction, where people read to gain knowledge and insights, not to be entertained.

Choose a few niche areas in which you've read more books than the average person. Make sure these are areas in which your target demographic would also be interested (i.e., you probably don't want to write book notes about masculinity if your target audience is young female executives).

Do more than just write summaries. Highlight what you found interesting and engaging. Write up key takeaways and whether or not you found the book or course worthwhile. Use your own rating system.

Publish each of these reviews as either posts or unlisted pages on your site. Create a new page labeled "Book/Course Notes" and link to new book and course notes as you publish them.

While reviews drive organic search traffic over time, you can co-opt existing audiences by using review posts as vicarious interviews with authors and instructors. When you find a resource particularly enjoyable or insightful, email the author or instructor a link of the review. Use a script like this one:

> Hi *[First name]*,
>
> My name is ***[your name]***, and I am ***[your positioning]*** who shares content at ***[your website]***.
>
> I wanted to let you know that I recently read and enjoyed ***[resource title]***. ***[Sincere compliment about what you enjoyed in the resource.]***
>
> I published my notes on the ***[resource]*** here: ***[URL]***. I thought it might be helpful for others who may consider reading it.
>
> Please feel free to share the notes—as well as any thoughts you might have.
>
> NRN—thanks for writing.
>
> *[Your name]*

NRN means "No reply necessary," and it's a way of telling readers that you know they are busy and you just wanted to drop them a line. It's one way to signal respect for their time.

Most authors and instructors won't reply. But a few will. And a few may share your notes with their own audiences. You just need a few authors or instructors with engaged audiences to share your notes to get in front of thousands of the right people.

This is also a relationship-building strategy so you can network with content creators you respect.

Learning curve: Low; just make sure to write helpful notes and not just summaries.

Recommended tools: FindThatLead (findthatlead.com) for finding the content creator's email address. Airtable (airtable.com) or Google Sheetsfor keeping track of outreach.

Quality of audience: Medium to high.

Example: nateliason.com/notes. Nat has 200+ detailed book notes, easily searchable and ordered by rating.

Extreme Niche Reporting and Expertise

Does your target audience value a high level of technical expertise? Do they place a premium on quality understanding of complex current events? Can you be one of the best and first people to make sense of news and developing situations?

If yes, you want to consider extreme niche reporting and expertise as a Brand Builder.

This works best if your positioning and target audience deal with technical matters that laypeople may find interest in but cannot easily understand. General fields of interest might be fitness niches (e.g., CrossFit), athletics (e.g., baseball analytics), policy (e.g., monetary policy), and law (e.g., Supreme Court rulings).

While you can always write on these topics, driving traffic requires an *urgency factor* (i.e., there are a lot of eyeballs on this topic *right now*) and a *believability factor* (i.e., can you credibly explain the subject to nonexperts?).

Stay on top of events related to your positioning and be one of the first people to break down what those events mean. Be one of the first out the door with quality teardowns and analyses on your personal site.

Connect directly with *established* industry experts and leaders by sending them your analyses as you publish them. Cite them when you can to give them a reason to engage.

If sending your analyses to other *experts*, ask for their feedback and input. If sending your analyses to *reporters* on your area of expertise, offer it for their reporting. Like with interviewing, use the Trading up the Chain strategy to connect with larger and larger experts and journalists. Do this consistently and you build a reputation as one of the go-to people on current events related to your positioning.

Learning curve: High. You have to know what you're talking about. This strategy works best for positioning and target audiences that value quick expertise.

Quality of audience: High.

Example: joshblackman.com. Josh built his brand around being one of the quickest and best Supreme Court watchers in the country.

Guest Blogging

Guest posting on other people's blogs is one of the most proven and respected ways to drive the right people to your site.

Other people have already done the work for you in building qualified audiences. Whether these are *blog* blogs (e.g., marginalrevolution.com), personal sites (e.g., penelopetrunk.com), or company sites (e.g., themuse.com), the people who run these sites *have an incentive* to publish high-quality work from other people. This saves time for them, puts a new post on their content calendar, and introduces their audience to a new and interesting person.

This means you can target people who are *just like you* in their positioning and not have to worry about "competition." Guest posting is collaboration, not competition.

Writing a killer guest post comes down to knowing your target audience well and developing a compelling Brand Builder Lead Magnet for the target audience. You can share a beautifully written post on a high-traffic site, but if it isn't what that audience needs when they read it, it might flop.

To get started guest posting, start with a list of bloggers and writers *you* enjoy who create content relevant to your positioning. Look for other people writing about what you write about.

Create a spreadsheet (like the one for interviews). Add columns for name, website, contact info, difficulty ("Easy," "Moderate," "Hard," "Reach"), mutual connections, pitches/ideas, and link to guest post standards. If all of the people on your list are "Hard" or "Reach" difficulty, search their sites for *other* people who guest posted. Add these people to your list—if they are guest posting on a "Hard" or "Reach" site, they're probably easier to access than the

"Hard" or "Reach" site itself. Do this until you have at least three bloggers or writers in each category.

Search on each person's site for guest post submission guidelines. Some bloggers have pages or posts saying what to do for them to consider a guest post (or if they consider them in the first place). If they have one, follow those instructions. If they don't, write down three unique pitches for each blogger that you believe their audience would enjoy. Look up the blogger's contact info. Send the person an email with the following information:

- Who you are
- What you write about
- Why you're reaching out to them
- Your three pitches for their site
- That you'll promote the post to your own audience
- That you'll send the post over in their preferred format (e.g., Google Doc, .txt file, Word doc)
- A clear ask if they would consider one of the three pitches

Here's an email script you can use:

> Subject Line: Guest Post for ***[Website]***?
>
> Hi ***[First name]***,
>
> My name is ***[Your name]*** and I am ***[your positioning]***. I've been a reader of yours since ***[year]*** and really enjoy your content. ***[Specific, sincere compliment about something their content has helped you with.]***
>
> I'm writing more on ***[topic]*** recently and would like to share a guest post for your site.
>
> [OPTIONAL: I recently published a post for ***[other blogger]*** that they really enjoyed. You can find it here: ***LINK***.]

As you develop a track-record of guest posts, cite them in new outreach emails. Give social proof and reduce the risk.

Here are three pitches I thought your audience might enjoy:

[Pitch 1]

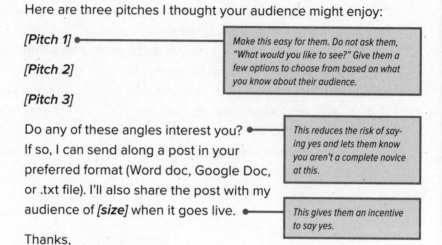

Make this easy for them. Do not ask them, "What would you like to see?" Give them a few options to choose from based on what you know about their audience.

[Pitch 2]

[Pitch 3]

Do any of these angles interest you? If so, I can send along a post in your preferred format (Word doc, Google Doc, or .txt file). I'll also share the post with my audience of ***[size]*** when it goes live.

This reduces the risk of saying yes and lets them know you aren't a complete novice at this.

This gives them an incentive to say yes.

Thanks,

[Your name]

This post is easy to reply to (they can answer, "Yes, the first pitch"), makes it clear you won't waste their time by doing something stupid like sending a PDF and gives them a variety of choices. It also makes it clear you aren't just sending the same pitch to dozens of different bloggers.

Once you get them to agree to a pitch, *then* write the post. Don't kill yourself writing a post before you get an editor or website owner to agree to an angle. While writing the post, write it as if speaking to somebody interested in your positioning but unfamiliar with you. Develop a Brand Builder Lead Magnet for the post that the other blogger's audience will feel *compelled* to click to your site to get. You can position it as a gift specifically for that audience. For example, if your positioning is that you're a sales professional who helps high-growth B2B companies scale quickly, you may write for another sales blogger whose audience is B2B executives and their sales teams. You might develop email scripts or a sales checklist that his readers can download on your website.

Take your time writing guest posts. Quality guest posts can take weeks to write but drive traffic for years after they go live. View the time you spend on a quality guest post as an investment.

Promote every new guest post you do to your audience. This sets you apart from most people who contribute guest posts and then expect the other writer to do all the work promoting the post.

> **Learning curve:** Moderate. A good guest post should take time, attention, and work. This Brand Builder is a lot easier if you enjoy writing.
>
> **Quality of audience:** High; *make sure your target audience reads blogs*. Some audiences, particularly younger people, prefer podcasts or vlogging to blogs.

Do Direct Research

As your audience grows, reach out to your email list and directly survey them about what websites they frequent, what kinds of media they enjoy, and to whom they listen. This takes the guesswork out of developing outreach lists.

Earned Media Contributing

You can contribute to publications online (e.g., *Business Insider, Fast Company, Entrepreneur*) without being a journalist or a professional columnist.

Most publications have writers called *contributors*. Contributors don't work for the publication. They're usually industry experts writing about specific issues from their perspective inside the business. Sometimes these contributors write one-off contributions (that are usually picked up from third-party sites like LinkedIn, Quora, or smaller publications), and sometimes they contribute regularly.

There are two ways to become a contributor to existing publications:

1. **Passive.** Create content on third-party sites that are trafficked by employees charged with finding new contributors. Hope they see your content and republish it.

2. **Active.** Directly approach these employees and pitch them on publishing your content.

The Passive Approach

Most publications have employees whose job it is to find high-quality content on the Internet and republish it on their publication. These employees spend their time on *other* sites that might be frequented by their own target audience. These sites can range from generic sites like Quora and Medium (medium.com) to LinkedIn and industry-specific publications. You can find which websites these employees hang out on by looking at *other* posts from contributors. Near the byline or the bio, you'll find a line that looks like this:

> This article was originally published on ***[website]***.

That tells you where the employee found the contributor's article.

These employees reverse-engineer Trading up the Chain for their jobs. As you write on smaller publications frequented by these employees, you may get republished in bigger outlets. Once you've been republished once, work on *building a relationship* with the employee who sourced your content. These tend to be junior employees without much sway, but they may leave to another publication or be promoted to editorial positions.

The Active Approach

Instead of passively hoping that employees and contributing editors find your articles and promote you to "contributor" status, actively search out people who can do this for you.

Actively approach these outlets by reaching out to and building relationships with editors and junior editors. Just like with guest posting, you want to *solve a problem* for the person you reach out to. Online editors and assistant editors usually have a quota of new articles they must publish every week or month. Some publications require that these articles be *original content* and not republished from elsewhere. On top of finding new content to publish, these editors are also usually writers themselves. In other words, they have full plates.

Take some of this work off their plates by pitching them on articles you'd like them to publish. Follow the same format for prospecting and pitching that you would for guest posting.

Credibility vs. Qualified Traffic

Journalistic publications usually have stricter standards about self-promotion than blogs do. These publications are better for driving *credibility* and allowing you to Trade up the Chain than they are for traffic. I know people who have driven better traffic from obscure bloggers with qualified audiences than they have from mainstream media websites.

Before investing in the time and energy required to land earned media, ask yourself, "What am I really trying to get out of this?" If you just want the credibility markers, go for it. If you're really focusing on traffic, it might be better to spend your time on other options.

As with guest posting, tell editors that you'll promote the article to your own audience. Drive traffic to *their* publication. Make *their* lives easier. Don't be creative. Just solve a problem for them.

The downsides with journalistic publishing are that you typically have to write original pieces (versus republishing old pieces) and must tone down self-promotion. The larger the publication, the longer the lead time. Don't plan on pitching an article one week and getting it published the next week.

Learning curve: Moderate. There's a whole game to pitching editors and writing pitches they like.

Quality of audience: Moderate to low. Major publications are better for credibility than traffic. You're also a victim of news cycles. A great piece that gets published the week a national story breaks might get less attention than a poor piece on a slow week.

Industry Publications and Earned Media

Your profession may have its own publications. These might be magazines, academic journals, reviews, websites, or human-interest publications. It might be *expected* of you that you publish or get featured in these publications (as in the case of academics). Or it may just be a laurel to rest on (as in the case of most professional publications).

If your target audience includes people in your profession, publishing regularly in professional publications sends a powerful signal that you stand apart from your peers.

There are primarily two types of industry publications: news-driven publications ("earned media") and research-driven publications. Which one you pursue depends on which one your target audience reads.

Landing Earned Media

Getting featured in news-driven publications requires long-term relationship-building and an understanding of the incentives facing industry journalists and editors.

Most professionals and companies approach landing media the wrong way: they have a newsworthy event related to their company or their career (e.g., an award, a big project, new funding, etc.), draft up a press release, and put the press release on websites designed for press releases. They *hope* an industry reporter finds it interesting enough to call them up and feature them in a publication.

This rarely works, especially when you're starting out..

Professionals and companies that regularly get featured in relevant media know they have to have a set of *go-to* journalists who *already* write about news related to their industry. They know that they have to build a relationship with journalists in a way that journalists *look forward* to emails from them with new news. And they know they have to couch their news in a way that the readers of the journalist's publication find interesting.

Here's a crazy example of the incentives facing journalists: Gawker Media. Gawker's New York City office featured a giant board ranking reporters against each other based on the number of clicks their articles got. Gawker's industry was gossip. Whichever reporters could find the juiciest gossip could produce articles with a viral factor. Others at the organization faced similar incentives to find the stories that made people want to click.

While Gawker is a vulgar example of click-driven journalism gone awry, all ad-driven publications face essentially the same set of incentives. They make their money either off of advertising or off of subscriptions. In either case, they want stories that make people *want* to visit the site. Speak to these incentives and journalists will listen.

Readers and reporters don't care about what *you* find interesting. What do *they* find interesting? What stories get the most traction? What angle can you work into your pitch so that journalists decide to speak with you?

PR professionals build out *media lists*. Media lists include the names, contact info, and publications of journalists who write on specific topics. For example, if you're a tech entrepreneur who wants to get attention for closing a fundraising round, have a media list of journalists who write about early stage startup fundraising.

You can buy media lists, inherit them from established friends and colleagues, or build out your own. Unless earned media in industry publications is a major component of your personal branding, I recommend just keeping a running spreadsheet that you can update with names as you come across new journalists. When you see articles that cover topics related to your positioning, make note of the name of the journalist who wrote the article, what publication it was in, and the journalist's contact info.

Make note of any unique or interesting *angles* the writer took. Is the story about entrepreneurship generally? Or is it about *women's* entrepreneurship? Is the story about local home construction? Or is it about *high-end* local home construction? Is the story about local bakers? Or is it about local *vegan, gluten-free* bakers?

Once you have a media list, find recent articles relevant journalists published related to your positioning. Come up with a unique angle that connects with the journalists' angle in their recent articles.

Draft them an email with these components:

- Who you are
- How you found them (e.g., old articles they've written)
- Why you're reaching out to them (i.e., what's newsworthy?)
- Why you think *they'd* be interested (i.e., why does your positioning and their positioning align? what angle are you taking?)
- An ask if they'd like to speak with you more about this topic

If your story has an element of timeliness to it, you can offer reporters what's called an *embargo.* This means they get exclusive rights to cover the story before anybody else.

Here's an email script you can use:

> Subject Line: Per your recent article on ***[subject]***
>
> Hi ***[First name]***,
>
> My name is ***[your name]***, and I am ***[your relevant positioning]***. I recently saw your article on ***[subject]***. ***[Sincere, specific compliment about what you liked about the article. The more detailed, the better. You want them to know you're reaching out to them and not just blasting the same email template to 100 reporters.]***
>
> I'm reaching out because I have a story that I think is relevant to you and your audience. ***[Your story and your angle tailored to this reporter.]***

Would covering this interest you? If so, I can send along some more info and times we can chat.

Thanks,

[Your name]

Optional: You can offer an "embargo" if the story is time-sensitive. Embargoes are exclusive rights you give to that journalist and publication to cover your story. If you don't have time-sensitive news, don't worry about this.

If journalists reply and say no, thank them for taking the time to follow up. *Then* ask them if they have a colleague who might be interested in your story. You can then email the colleague with a subject line like,

Per *[original journalist's name].*

For long-term relationship-building, offer to act as a source on topics related to your positioning for the journalist. This means journalists can come to you for quotations or information when writing a story related to what you know. Reaching out as a source or an expert on topics related to their beat is a great way to start a relationship with journalists.

Learning curve: Low. Build out your media list and Trade up the Chain. This strategy takes time, patience, and relationship-building to work well.

Example: Haley Hoffman Smith, author of *Her Big Idea*, got her self-published book featured in *Entrepreneur* magazine and *The Weekly Standard* using this strategy.*

Research-Driven Publications

If you work in a research-driven field like law or academia, publishing in journals elevates your status among your peers and drives small but highly targeted traffic to your personal site.

---

* For more on Haley's approach, see zakslayback.com/case-study-how-to-pitch-journalists/

Your field's journals have their own standards and customs for submitting articles for publication. What's important to consider from a personal branding perspective is how your articles build your brand and your positioning. A few unique and pointed journal articles can establish you as *the* go-to person in your field on the subject matter. Choose a sufficiently small niche in your field that you won't be competing with everybody else. Write articles that are both timeless and evergreen but speak to contemporary concerns.

Focus on being prolific in this niche. It probably only takes a few well-written articles to set you apart from 90 percent of the authors in your niche. Develop these angles separately and submit papers to appropriate journals. In most research-driven fields, the reputation of the journal matters more than the number of papers. Take this into consideration while writing.

Link to the papers on your website when they go live and publish original posts (for search engine purposes) featuring the papers and links.

> **Learning curve:** High. You need to know what you're writing about, and you need to know the style of choice for your profession.

> **Example:** Jason Brennan, a professor at Georgetown University, writes on arguments against democracy, a small but noteworthy niche. See Jason's article, "Productive in Publishing," on producing in research-driven fields like academia.*

Launching Your Own Podcast

Podcasting is blogging for people who don't like blogging.

Podcasting gives you an excuse to talk to interesting people, get them to share your work, and get introductions to even more interesting people. A well-executed podcast alone can build your entire

* Jason Brennan, "Productive in Publishing," Daily Nous, November 10, 2019, dailynous.com/2016/11/10/productive-publishing-guest-post-jason-brennan/.

personal brand. One of the personal brand success stories later in this chapter built his own dream job and launched his company through podcasting.

The key to podcasting well is positioning and consistency. Most podcasters stop publishing after just a few episodes because they expect to get massive audiences overnight. Just like with a blog, it takes time to build an audience for a podcast. People won't just stumble into your podcast on a podcasts app. They have to be sent there by people they already trust and like.

Successfully launching a podcast, then, is an audio-based cousin of doing interviews on your blog.

Before Launching the Podcast

Develop a plan for how you'll start and promote your podcast. A plan helps you stay accountable to your ambition with launching the podcast and develop the habits that will make it successful. Podcasting is far too time-intensive to enter without some kind of plan.

Choose unique positioning that gives your target audience reason to listen and your target guests reason to join you.

Make a list of guests you'd like to have on the show, start reaching out, and Trade up the Chain to bigger and bigger guests. Your Cabinet of Models is one place to start for accessible guests. Most successful podcasts start with the hosts interviewing their friends and mentors.

Follow the same spreadsheet organization system for interviewing guests on your blog. Find previous examples of podcast interviews with guests before you invite them on. Just because people are fluent in the written word doesn't mean they're good at interviewing. You want guests people want to *listen* to.

Unlike email interviews, podcast interviews have to be scheduled and are time-consuming. Your email outreach to potential guests should signal that you won't waste their time. Do this by having a specific reason for why you want to interview them, give past examples of interviews you've done, and be straightforward in your ask in the email.

Here's a script you can use for emailing people you don't know:

> Hi *[name]*,
>
> My name is ***[your name]***, and I am the host of ***[your podcast name]***, a podcast about ***[something relevant to their positioning]***. I'd like to invite you to join our show. I found you on ***[platform, media, other podcast]***.
>
> Our target audience would be interested in your work with ***[very specific, cited example of why they are relevant to your show]***.
>
> *When looking for examples of their work you can cite, don't just go for the most recent post or article. That looks lazy. Go back a few weeks or months.*
>
> We're just launching the podcast, so our listenership is still growing, but our listeners are mostly ***[description of your listeners]***. I know you're very busy, so I'd understand if you had to decline.
>
> Would this interest you? Interviews are typically *[x]* minutes long and are conducted via ***[Skype, Zoom, phone, etc.]***.
>
> *This gives them an idea of how costly it is to say yes.*
>
> Thank you,
>
> ***[Your name]***

Once guests confirm, send them a calendar invite letting them know how you'll contact them and what you'll cover in the show.

Recording the Interviews

The most important factors for quality podcast interviews are:

1. **Quality of the guest.** Great audio quality and a great host can't make up for a terrible guest.
2. **Quality of the host.** Don't interrupt your guests while they speak, and don't go on long, rambling tirades.

3. **Audio quality.** Get a quality microphone (such as a Blue Yeti USB microphone, which costs about $130) and a high-speed Wi-Fi connection, and record your guests through a platform like zoom.us or Skype. Ask guests to use a microphone and call in from a computer in a quiet location. Avoid echoey locations—echo is difficult to remove in editing.
4. **Show notes and description.** Give people reading the blog post with the podcast embedded a little bit of info about the episode. Link to any books or resources mentioned in the episode. Give people something they can share without actually having to share the direct podcast link.

Let the guest guide the conversation. Treat your questions like mere guardrails that keep the guest from veering too far off course. Until you have a large personal following, your listeners listen *to hear the guests speak*, not to hear you speak. Remember, you grow your audience by interviewing guests who have their own audiences. You are merely a way for the guest's audience to hear the guest speak.

Decide how often you'll publish it (every other day, weekly, biweekly? Try not to make it less often than biweekly.) and record at least five episodes before launching. You don't want to run around at the last second trying to get interviews scheduled so that you don't fall off your rhythm.

After the Interview

After the interview, add intros and outros for the interview and clean up audio quality. Your intro or outro should include a call to action telling listeners to visit your website, subscribe, and rate the podcast.

Don't worry *too* much about audio quality at first. You'll have more time and resources to improve as you gain experience. Go listen to early episodes of *The Tim Ferriss Show* and *The Joe Rogan Experience*. They're awful compared to the high-production episodes produced years into the show. Don't let perfectionism keep you from starting.

Do, Delegate, Schedule, Eliminate

Recall the Urgent/Important matrix from Chapter 2. Is it necessary that *you* do the editing? Consider hiring a virtual assistant through a service like Upwork (upwork.com) to do the time-intensive editing after the interview is done.

Send guests an email thanking them and letting them know when you plan on publishing the interview. Ask them for an introduction to *two* other people they know who may make great guests. Give them parameters on what makes a great guest. How old are the people? What industry do they work in? What's their experience? What's their story? Make it *easy* for the guest to suggest names.

Publishing the Interview

Publish the interview through a platform that distributes both to Apple Podcasts and to either Spotify or a major Android podcast platform (e.g., Stitcher).

Separately publish each interview as its own blog post on your website. Include the guest's name in the title and details about the guest in the body of the post. Link to any resources the guest mentioned during the show.

Email guests letting them know the interview is live, thanking them for their time again, and asking them to share the interview with their audience. Give them a suggested angle for why you think their audience will enjoy the interview.

Repeat this process and Trade up the Chain to bigger guests.

Learning curve: Moderate. Starting a podcast used to be hard and stressful. There are now so many resources available online that once you develop the skill of interviewing well, starting a podcast only takes a few hours.

Recommended tools: Use Buzzsprout (buzzsprout.com) as a podcast hosting service. Create cover art either on your own at Canva (canva.com) or hire a designer through Fiverr (fiverr.com). Use zoom.us to record interviews. Use Audacity (audacityteam.org) to edit interviews. Unless you love audio production, you can outsource this later.

Example: Molly Beck (messybun.com) used a podcast to help her land her dream job and continues to podcast today as part of her own business. Molly's book *Reach Out* has step-by-step instructions on how to send emails to prospective professional contacts.

Appearing on *Other* People's Podcasts

Being featured on a single episode of a podcast with qualified audience can drive more engagement than a feature on the national news.

Landing interviews on podcasts takes time, relationship-building, and an understanding of what the podcast hosts look for in guests. Established podcast hosts have guest backlogs for months and typically won't respond to cold requests from random people telling them, "feature me on your show!" They *will* consider guest recommendations from their own listeners and from other podcast hosts they know and trust.

New podcast hosts and those who have yet to break through the noise *constantly* struggle with finding guests and keeping their interview queues filled. For them, a cold email from a qualified, eloquent person asking to join their show solves a problem.

Successfully landing a podcast tour is a success story in Trading up the Chain. Start with these new, junior podcasters and trade up through introductions and cold emails to larger podcasters. This is just like guest posting.

Identify a set of podcasts you'd like to be interviewed on. Make sure the audience of the podcast fits your own target audience.

It's not unusual to find a pyramid of podcasters behind podcasting superstars (e.g., Tim Ferriss, Joe Rogan). Some of *their* guests have podcasts of their own. And *these* podcast hosts have guests who *also* have podcasts. You won't land an interview with a podcast superstar (at first), so work your way backward through their guests to find approachable guests.

Pitching Podcast Hosts

Pitching podcast hosts through cold email isn't easy. You want to signal all the right traits and not look like a random person just trying to get attention. Here's a breakdown of a great cold pitch to a podcast host: zakslayback.com/interview-on-a-podcast/.

Once you land the podcast interview and get it on the calendar, develop a Brand Builder Lead Magnet for the podcast's listeners. Compel them to go to your website, get your Brand Builder Lead Magnet, and join your own audience.

After the podcast interview goes live and the podcaster gauges feedback from her audience, ask for two introductions to other podcasters she knows. If you land three interviews with junior podcasters and they each introduce you to two people, each of which interviews you, you have nine podcast interviews in a short time.

Learning curve: Low; the hardest part is making a cold pitch.

Quality of audience: Low at first, but compounds quickly.

Starting Your Own Vlog

Some target audiences spend more time on YouTube and video sites than they do reading blogs or listening to podcasts. If this is how your target audience consumes information and you don't mind appearing on camera, start a vlog.

Vlogging follows the same fundamentals as starting a podcast. Do not assume you'll get traffic without partnering with and featuring other people. Do not assume people will just *find* your vlog. And, do not assume people subscribe and share without being told to subscribe and share.

Video and audio quality matter for vlogs, just like audio quality matters for podcasts. Plan to spend at least twice as much time editing a vlog as you would a podcast.

To get started vlogging, follow the same strategy you would for launching a podcast. Emphasize telling stories, featuring other people, and engaging the audience directly. Successful examples of vlogging build a sense of community among the viewers and directly ask for their feedback and input.

> **Learning curve:** High. This is something I only recommend pursuing if you enjoy the process of making the vlog. While you can outsource some editing to a VA, vlogging is still a time-consuming and high-investment activity.
>
> **Recommended tools:** Camera: Canon PowerShot G7X Mark II. A high-quality smartphone camera will work at first. Software: Adobe Premiere Pro.
>
> **Example:** Jon Shanahan (theKavalier.com) runs a men's style vlog reviewing clothes, shoes, and accessories from his Pittsburgh, Pennsylvania, home.

Side-Projects and Mini Products

Build products that your target audience finds valuable and that set you apart from everybody else just putting out commentary and content.

Launching products signals not only that you know what your target audience needs but that you can provide it. Engaging products take on a brand of their own and land Brand Builders like earned media and guest posting opportunities. They also allow you to *complement* your personal brand without tying it entirely to one subject matter or area of expertise.

Think of products like Brand Builder Lead Magnets on steroids. If you build one, you still need to drive traffic to it. I recommend building your own personal brand audience to at least 1,000 subscribers before building a product. That way, when the product launches, you have a core audience you can launch it to.

Unlike with personal branding, entire niches of the Internet exist solely to support and promote products. Product Hunt (ProductHunt.com) helps users find and promote products they find interesting. Products range from apps and physical products to e-books and courses. A well-positioned launch on Product Hunt can provide the brand building that a product needs.

A single Product Hunt launch can drive more than 1,000 qualified subscribers to the product. Then engage with the product subscribers as you would your personal brand subscribers.

Learning curve: High. There's a whole art and science to mini-product launches. And that doesn't even take into account actually *building* the product. This is a Brand Builder I only recommend once you've established your personal brand. You could read entire books on this subject alone.

Recommended tools: Product Hunt (ProductHunt.com) gives you a unique and captive audience to launch to if your positioning aligns with theirs.

Quality of audience: High.

Example: fantasySCOTUS.net. Fantasy football for Supreme Court watchers. This is a product spun out by Josh Blackman (joshblackman.com) as a side-project while clerking for judges. Josh stacked two talents to launch FantasySCOTUS: knowing about the Supreme Court and basic software development.

Social Media (with a Unique Take)

Most people use social media in the wrong way when building their personal brand.

They build a website, write a few articles, maybe record some audio or video content, and share it on social media waiting for the *flood* of new traffic.

And . . . . crickets.

This is the personal branding equivalent of blasting out the same résumés when trying to get a job or going to networking events and leaving your business card for people to pick up. It makes sense on its face, but it ends up being a distraction from the real work you have to do to generate results.

Social media is a personal branding distraction for most people. They'd be better off spending their time doing outreach and focusing on other Brand Builders.

Some people bring a unique voice, story, and understanding of their audiences that lets them use social media instead of being used by social media.

Successfully using social media requires a few things:

- **Understanding of your target audience and what they want.** Which platforms do they spend time on? What kind of content are they looking for?
- **Authenticity and a unique take.** People see through social media talking heads pretty quickly. This is harder for most people than they realize.
- **Consistency.** Most social media platforms are not designed for depth of engagement. They're designed for clicks and attention. Double down on what works in your messaging and stay at the front of users' minds.

Even if you succeed at driving engagement on social media through likes, shares, retweets, etc., *consistently* push your audience to go to your personal site and join your email list. A simple tweak of a newsfeed algorithm or an unexpected banning can tank your audience on most social media platforms. Use it as a feeder, but don't use it as your only feeder.

Becoming a Social Media Pro

If it does make sense for you to use social media as a Brand Builder, take the time to *research* what works best on which platform. Social media platforms often prioritize certain kinds of content and use complex and opaque algorithms to do so.

For example, LinkedIn is notorious for changing its newsfeed algorithm. At one point, it prioritized long-form, blog-like content.

Then it prioritized story-like posts with short sentences written on each line, boosting people who posted often. Then it prioritized video content. Then it prioritized content from people who don't post often. Instead of trying to stay on top of every change yourself, outsource your expertise at first.

Consider hiring a teacher or gaining an advisor who knows the social media platform of your choice. Learn from this expert what kinds of content succeeds on that platform and why. Ask what pitfalls you should avoid and why.

Here's a script you can use to hire a teacher who knows a platform well:

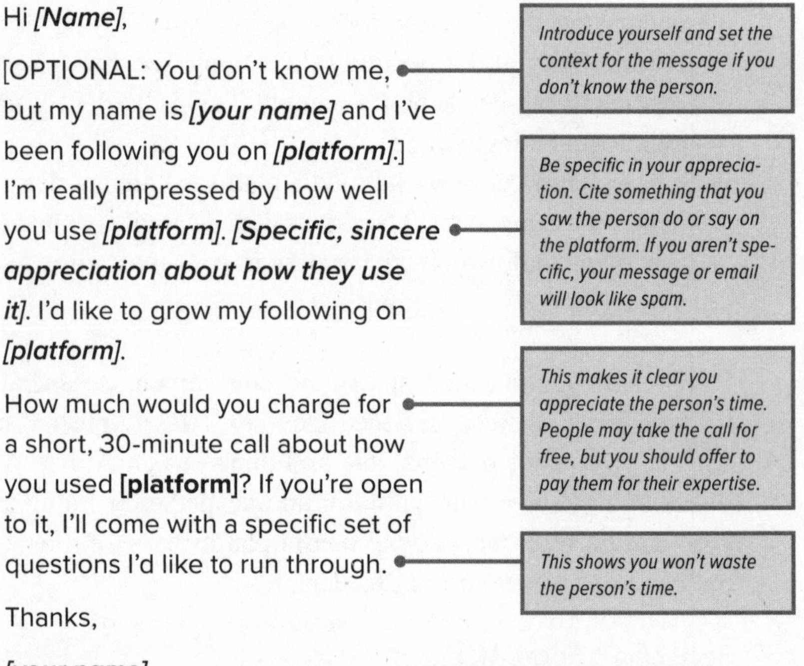

Hi *[Name]*,
[OPTIONAL: You don't know me, but my name is ***[your name]*** and I've been following you on ***[platform]***.] I'm really impressed by how well you use ***[platform]***. ***[Specific, sincere appreciation about how they use it]***. I'd like to grow my following on ***[platform]***.
How much would you charge for a short, 30-minute call about how you used **[platform]**? If you're open to it, I'll come with a specific set of questions I'd like to run through.
Thanks,
[your name]
Introduce yourself and set the context for the message if you don't know the person.
Be specific in your appreciation. Cite something that you saw the person do or say on the platform. If you aren't specific, your message or email will look like spam.
This makes it clear you appreciate the person's time. People may take the call for free, but you should offer to pay them for their expertise.
This shows you won't waste the person's time.

Use this call as a way to answer specific questions about gaining traction on a platform. Dig into technicalities as much as you can—what kinds of posts are prioritized? How often should you post? Who should you target? Should you tag other people? How should you follow others?

Learning curve: High. Most people who try to take off on social media fail. It takes a lot of trial and error and knowing your audience to get it right. Understand your opportunity cost before pursuing social media. Is your time better spent elsewhere?

Quality of audience: Variable. It depends on the platform and your engagement.

Example: Ed Latimore (@edlatimore) built a large and dedicated following on Twitter through consistently and authentically sharing his insights from growing up in the projects of Pittsburgh, getting sober, becoming a boxer, and studying physics. Ed is also a good example of Scott Adams's talent stack (see Chapter 6).

Virtual Conferences

Virtual conferences are collections of prerecorded webinars with yourself and other speakers, advertised to attendees to watch at their leisure. They involve a fraction of the cost that running real-life conferences does and provide evergreen benefit.

Before Launching

To run your own virtual conference, start with a theme and a list of ideal speakers you'd like to invite. Follow an operating procedure similar to the one for inviting podcast guests. You want speakers who are verbally proficient, are believable, and have their own audiences they can attract to the conference.

Start by inviting medium-tier guests with large enough audiences to drive registrations. As you drive interest in the event, use registration numbers as an incentive to invite top-tier guests. Give guests the opportunity to pitch attendees through their own unique value propositions. Guests join for the opportunity to drive traffic to their own sites. Give them reason to join by showing them how much interest you've generated.

Once you have a few medium-tier guests confirmed, announce the event with its own landing page and an announcement to your own email list. Ask confirmed guests to do the same.

While you can save the talks for use in the future, limit public access to just a few days. This is a sales technique called *scarcity* and is proven to increase sign-up rates.

Should I Charge for the Conference?

You can charge to access the talks at any time outside of the conference window. Pricing introduces new technical complexity to running the virtual conference, but it can provide a nice incentive to drive engagement.

If you're going to charge a price, consider having a free tier and a premium tier. Premium tier gives access to the talks at any point. Free tier gives access only during the designated conference days.

Prerecord all of the talks via zoom.us. Write up notes from each talk and ask speakers if they'd like to send along sign-up bonuses (unique value propositions that you can advertise as a bonus for signing up for the conference).

Launching

Email attendees at these intervals:

- Several days before the launch of the conference reminding them to put it on their calendar
    - *You can also ask them here to refer friends to the event.*
- The day before the launch of the conference
- During the launch of each session, letting them know the talks are live
- After the event asking them to fill out a post-event survey for feedback on the speakers

- Optional: If you're charging for lifetime access, email free registrants after the event advertising a last-second opportunity to upgrade to lifetime access. Some will have missed the event and will take you up on this offer.

  Learning curve: High. This is an advanced Brand Builder and one I only recommend for somebody who has patience, some technical understanding of WordPress, and an existing email list.

  Recommended tools: While most of what you need to run a virtual conference *can* be built on WordPress with plug-ins and Wistia, Virtual Summits (virtualsummits.com) provides a full-stack solution. You'll also want to use zoom.us to record the talks and Mailchimp to track and notify attendees.

  Quality of audience: High.

  Example: menofcharacter.app.virtualsummits.com. Bill Masur's Men of Character conference drove more than 1,100 attendees and top-tier speakers from across the Internet.

Personal Brand Events

Your personal brand dominates your personal brand for good reason. The time and energy you invest in building your personal brand carries itself both to people you don't know locally (through the Internet) and people you do know locally.

You should still take the time to build out your brand locally. Do this for four reasons:

1. **Don't compete. Grow.** You may not be the best sales professional in the country, but you may be one of the best in Portland. You may not be the best gluten-free baker in the country, but you may be the best in Austin. You may not be the best photographer in the country, but you may be one of the best in Pittsburgh. Consistently aim to compete with as small a group as possible. This lets you focus on growing your skills

and your unique positioning instead of focusing on the biggest competition.

2. **Grow your local network.** Don't neglect your local network when looking to grow your target audience. Your next big project, business partner, or investor could be in your backyard. You don't know what you don't know about your local network.
3. **Build collateral for your personal brand.** Your personal brand should show that you do actually exist in the real world. Photos and videos of workshops, talks, and events you've worked at locally lend credibility for visitors who may want to hire you for similar events.
4. **Capture local star power.** Capturing local star power helps you persuade others to work with you. That others can point to you and say, "He's one of the best in town on [your positioning]" is often all you need to land new opportunities. You can't capture this star power without working locally.

Use these local Brand Builders to establish yourself as a go-to person for your positioning.

Speak at Local Universities or Companies

Most universities welcome guest speakers from the local community. You neither have to be a PhD nor an alum of the university to get a professor or club to welcome you as a guest speaker. You just have to be credible enough to interest the students.

Speaking at a university brings three distinct advantages to your personal brand:

1. **Credibility.** You can now say that [X] University has hosted you as a speaker.
2. **Audience.** If your target audience includes educated young adults, speaking at a college puts you directly in front of your audience. Bring a sign-up sheet and ask students to join your email list to stay in touch.

3. **Collateral.** Some professors allow you to record your talk. Bring a small tripod and a smartphone to record.

Before the Talk

Start by identifying the department or clubs that would host you. If you're positioned as a sales expert, you'll want to look at the business school and business clubs. If you're positioned as a legal expert, you'll want to look at the law school and law clubs.

Then, look at the classes in each department to determine which makes the most sense to approach. A good rule of thumb is that you want to approach professors and instructors who teach more than just entry-level courses. Most entry-level courses have fixed syllabi and no extra days allotted for guest speakers.

Using LinkedIn and Facebook, see if you have mutual connections with the instructor. If you do, ask for an introduction. If not, use this email script:

> Hi ***[Dr./Prof./Mr./Ms. Last Name]***,
>
> My name is ***[your name]***, and I am a ***[your positioning]*** here in ***[your city]***. I'm taking the time to do guest lectures at local universities and schools and wanted to reach out to you and offer to give a talk to your ***[subject]*** students.
>
> ***[Recommended: Social proof or credibility that you've spoken at other schools, companies, or organizations. Give them reason to take you seriously.]***
>
> I'm also volunteering to do one-on-one office hours with students interested in ***[your positioning]***.
>
> Is this something you'd be interested in? If so, I can follow up with some more info and we can put a date on the calendar.
>
> Thanks,
>
> ***[Your name]***

You just need one instructor at a university to say yes for you to get in the door at that school. Once you get a talk scheduled, send a reminder email one day before the talk confirming that you'll join the class.

If approaching a student group, ask if you can speak at one of their meetings. Most student group presidents welcome a new guest speaker if there's time in the calendar. Don't worry about requesting a speaking fee until you've already established your brand as a professional speaker.

Target student groups that are part of larger national and international organizations. You can then use the fact that you spoke to X student group at Y University as an in for speaking to X student group at Z University.

During the Talk

Focus your talk on real-world examples. One of the reasons college instructors bring in guest lecturers is to expose students to professionals who are *already in* the industry and not just instructors at a college.

Most college students don't want to be lectured *at*. Use no more than 75 percent of your time to give the actual talk. Engage students through question-and-answer to make an impact both on the students and on the instructor.

At the end of the talk, give a student a sign-up sheet to pass around the class. This sheet should include their names and email addresses. Use this information to stay in touch with the students. Actually ask a student to pass the paper around. If you just put it on the front desk and tell students to walk up to it to join your email list, you may get a few sign-ups. You'll get more if you ask them to pass it around.

After the Talk

Follow up with the students who signed your sheet within 48 hours. Congratulate them on staying in touch with you and send along any specific information you mentioned to them.

Type up your notes from your talk. Publish these notes on your website. Make note that you gave them as a talk at the specific university at which you spoke.

Send a thank you note to the instructor (physical notes make a bigger impression than email). Offer to meet with the instructor over coffee or lunch if you did not while visiting. A single guest lecture can turn into a regular appearance with proper relationship-building.

Upload your slides (if you used slides) and embed them in the post. If you recorded the talk, upload the video to a video hosting site and embed this in the post, too.

Now you have a piece of collateral that you can send to *other* instructors as evidence that you can give a great guest lecture.

Learning curve: Low.

Recommended tools: For video hosting, use YouTube, Vimeo (vimeo.com), or Wistia (wistia.com). For sharing your slides, use SlideShare (slideshare.net).

Quality of audience: Variable. Don't assume your best audiences will be at the most prestigious universities. Your best audiences will be in classes that best fit your positioning. Some of my best audiences have been at small, obscure colleges. Some of my worst audiences have been at prestigious Ivy League universities.

Host Your Own Workshop or Event

Consider hosting your own workshop or event to both engage your existing local network and establish yourself as an expert in your field. Running large conferences and events is *hard*. Events involve not just logistics and scheduling but marketing, sales, communication, and nonstop engagement before and after the event. Put together your own Cabinet of Models and an ROK plan before heading down this path.

That being said, *successfully* hosting an event or workshop doesn't just establish your credibility in your subject matter. It also signals competence and conscientiousness far above the norm and gives you reason to build relationships with high-profile individuals (if you are bringing in other speakers).

Start Small

If you've never hosted an event before, start small with a workshop at work or a local community center aimed at no more than 25 attendees.

Most employers jump at the opportunity to give their employees professional development training. Pitch your boss on letting you run a workshop on something you know well and that other employees would benefit from learning. This doesn't even have to be *directly* related to your job. Employers want employees to believe that the company values their well-being. It's not unusual for companies to host workshops on personal finance, relationships, communication, and other life skills.

Advertise the benefit of attending the workshop directly in the title. If your positioning is as a dating expert, advertise a workshop on, "Saving Your Relationship Before It Goes Downhill" instead of "The Major Relationship Dynamics that Lead to Failure."

Follow an operating procedure similar to that for hosting a guest lecture at a university. Actively solicit email addresses from attendees, follow up shortly afterward, and engage those who signed up directly. Get direct feedback on how you can improve the workshop and what they would like to see more of in the future. Record your workshop and publish what you can on your personal site.

If demand for additional workshops persists, consider launching a workshop series.

Trade up from here to larger and larger workshops. You may consider hosting workshops with other speakers. Do this internally or with major corporate sponsors.

Host Your Own Parties or Dinners

You don't have to host workshops, do guest lectures, and put yourself out there to build your brand with fun local events. Consider hosting invite-only parties and dinners as a way to engage your local network and meet new people.

This is also a low-cost, informal way to remind your existing network that they know you and can engage with you, even if you have no reason otherwise to speak with them.

Host invite-only dinners or parties with people you *want* to be around and get to know better. Deputize attendees with the opportunity to invite one or two other people like them to join you. If you invite 5 people who each invite 2 people, you have 15 attendees with relatively little work.

Like most networking-related activities, doing this well comes down to making the experience feel authentic and not transactional. Don't brand it as anything in particular. Don't advertise it as a "happy hour" or a "networking event." Emphasize the role in coming together as interesting people and sharing food.

Start by inviting a few close friends so that you have a minimum turnout confirmed. Then, invite acquaintances you'd like to see there.

Here's an email script you can use to invite an acquaintance you don't know well enough to text or message on social media:

> Hi *[First name]*,
>
> I'm hosting a dinner/party with some friends in the area on *[date]* and I'd like to invite you to join us. The other guests are all ***[whatever you all have in common. Are you entrepreneurs? Young professionals? Creatives?]*** in the *[your city]* area. There are a few that I think you'd really enjoy meeting.
>
> Are you interested in attending? If so, I can send along more info on location and food.
>
> *[Your name]*
>
> PS—I really enjoyed ***[recent post, article, or content this person put out and a sincere compliment about it]***.

Learning curve: Low. As you get better at this, you can make the events larger and even turn them into fund-raisers.

Quality of audience: Extremely high.

Example: Sol Orwell (sjo.com and examine.com) hosts food-based events really well. Sol hosts both invite-only entrepreneur dinners in Toronto and larger invite-only fund-raisers that have raised more than $100,000 for nonprofit causes. Read more here: www.sjo.com/dinners/.

PERSONAL BRAND SUCCESS STORIES

Your personal brand accelerates your professional and personal goals by signaling your skills, knowledge, and positive traits to an extended network. This works for starting your career, changing careers, building a side business, or just hitting your professional goals faster.

Here are some of my favorite examples I've seen, met, worked with, and learned from. These interviews are available on ZakSlayback.com/book/pbinterviews.

Success Story: Josh Blackman (JoshBlackman.com)

Profession: Legal scholar

Main content: Blogging

Josh Blackman is one of the country's leading constitutional law scholars on issues of technology and of Obamacare. He's also my first mentor. He taught me from a young age the power of owning and crafting your personal brand.

Josh started his website as a college student at Penn State as a side business and later as a blog. After arriving at George Mason University Law School (now the Antonin Scalia School of Law), he focused his writing on constitutional law topics. His doubled down on issues such as privacy and Supreme Court watching.

Josh became known as one of the quickest and most prolific analysts on Supreme Court opinions. He launched the Harlan Institute and Fantasy SCOTUS (FantasySCOTUS.net and FantasySCOTUS .org, with which I helped) as an offshoot of his own personal brand as a Supreme Court watcher. This helped as a Brand Builder when it caught the attention of popular legal bloggers.

He did all of this while working a full-time job as a law clerk for federal judges. He eventually landed two book deals on the legal status of the Patient Protection and Affordable Care Act (Obamacare) and is a regular speaker on issues of constitutional law around the country.

Legal academia places a high importance on pedigree. Few tenure-track positions are offered *anywhere* every year, and most go to graduates of Harvard, Yale, or Princeton. Josh set himself apart from his peers by doubling down on what he was good at and carving out a strong, if not niche, positioning. The opportunities he generated through his personal brand, combined with his professional experience, helped him land a tenured position as a law professor at the South Texas College of Law.

What I like most about Josh's personal brand story is that it shows you don't have to do anything sleazy or "digital marketing-y" to build out a *strong* personal brand. You just need to focus on what you're good at, ignore what you're not, and become prolific. Josh's reputation as an expert grew as a function of his ability to focus relentlessly on what he wanted to study. Much of personal branding success just comes down to focusing on your positioning long enough to outlast others in your space. Those you don't outlast become collaborators rather than competitors.

Success Story: Kelly Hackmann (KellyHackmann.com and innocentideas.com)

Profession: Startup sales and customer success professional

Main content: Blogging

Kelly Hackmann works remotely for a startup as a sales and customer support professional. He landed that job despite having limited sales or startup for experience.

What made Kelly stand out to the vice president of sales was his website (InnocentIdeas.com), where he wrote regularly. Specifically, a post he wrote on the importance of sales (www.innocentideas.com/2016/10/08/sales-or-fails/) and how he approaches a process of constant pitching and rejection. He had no other remarkable experience or skills that made him stand apart from his equally qualified competitors.

The VP of sales jumped on hiring him once he saw this post. Most candidates had little idea what the sales process was like. Few made it more than a couple of months due to the grueling psychological nature of rejection. But here was somebody coming to it with clear eyes, a level head, and a mature approach. *That's* somebody worth talking to.

Kelly's sites give an example of using your personal brand as more than just, "I know X and can do Y." He signaled more than skills. He signaled *positive traits and characteristics.* His writing wasn't just about a topic that *the right people* wanted to read about, it was well-written and mature.

You don't need to be a business owner or even an expert to benefit from building and crafting your own personal brand. You want a hub of collateral signaling positive traits about yourself so that when the right opportunity comes along, you're prepared.

That's what a tailored and maintained brand does for you.

Success Story: Vanessa Musi (VanessaMusi.com)

Profession: Business owner and baker

Main content: Recipes

Vanessa Musi is a baker and business owner based in Austin, Texas. She's not *simply* a baker, though. Vanessa's positioning appeals to people interested in healthy baked goods like paleo, gluten-free, and low sugar. Even more, she further focuses her positioning by appealing to a Spanish-speaking population.

Vanessa's positioning helps her stand out and know *exactly* what kinds of content to post, where to post it, and whom to advertise to. Her credibility markers speak exactly to her target audience—people who care about healthy foods: Whole Foods, Starbucks, Bulletproof, and KitchenAid jump out.

How would these credibility markers look different if her positioning were different?

While Vanessa has an entire business built around her baked goods (Noble Baking, LLC), her *personal* brand lets her amplify what her business does beyond its own brand. People don't just buy for her food and her recipes. They buy for what *she* stands for—healthy baked goods accessible to English and Spanish speakers alike.

The difference between an effective and useful personal brand and an ineffective and fluffy one comes down to positioning backed by evidence. Know those you can help, how you can help them, and show them that you can actually help them.

Success Story: Aaron Watson (GoingDeepWithAaron.com)

Profession: Business owner, previously sales professional

Main content: Podcasting and vlogging

Aaron Watson started his podcast *Going Deep with Aaron Watson* right out of college. He interviewed entrepreneurs, authors, professionals, and politicians while working a large corporate sales job. A few years out of school, the connections and brand he built through *Going Deep* let him launch his own creative marketing company and host his own conference, the Going Deep Summit.

Aaron started with what little professional experience he had: sales experience. He interviewed people on how to get better at salesand how to use social media platforms like Snapchat for business. He also just reached out to authors and thinkers he thought were interesting. In time, this let him expand his guest base and pursue his interests outside of what he worked on and studied.

Aaron wasn't an expert in anything when he got started. Podcasting gave him an excuse to reach out to busy people whom he otherwise would have never gotten in touch with. Eventually, he built up enough episodes to land some dream guests and lead marketing for an even larger podcaster.

Aaron's personal brand is a reminder that you don't have to be an *expert* at anything to start adding value to other people's days. Young professionals tend to either jump too quickly into building out a personal brand before they've built anything, or they hold off for too long thinking they have to be an expert to start building.

Start building. Focus on substance and delivering value to others—through products, experience, services, or content—and your personal brand follows from there. *Going Deep with Aaron Watson* gives a great example of that.

Success Story: Hannah Phillips (HannahPhillipsMedia.com)

Profession: Artist, photographer, and business owner

Main content: Photography and vlogging

Hannah Phillips started creating art while still in high school. She learned photography on the side after school and started a side business taking photos for local events and for graduating seniors. She chose not to go to college and instead worked full-time on her business.

Hannah's brand caught the attention of local clubs, companies, and individuals who hired her for photography and original art. Instead of hiding behind a sterile company brand, she combined her personal brand with her business and let the positive traits about her business become part of her local reputation and vice versa.

This helped Hannah land several job offers from creative agencies for jobs that otherwise required college degrees. She later joined Aaron Watson (above) and started her own creative agency at 20.

The important lesson from Hannah's brand is that even if you just have a side business or even a full-time business, there are long-term career benefits to cultivating your own personal brand. Her top-tier photography skills and ability to show up and make clients love her weren't just *the company*, they were part of *working with her.* Together, Aaron and Hannah combined this approach of blending personal and professional brands by creating buzz for their company, Piper Creative (PiperCreative.co), with a vlog series documenting the stress and victories of starting a company.

Success Story: Ed Latimore (EdLatimore.com and @edlatimore)

Profession: Physics tutor, chess player, writer, and business owner

Main content: Tweets and blog posts

Ed Latimore grew up in some of Pittsburgh's toughest projects. He went on to become a boxer, join the National Guard, and then attend college and study physics (years after most people enroll in college) and built a cult following on Twitter.

Ed's an example of building a truly *personal* brand. His Twitter followers follow *for him, his stories, and his experience.* While he may occasionally go into tactics and details on boxing, physics, chess, or learning another language, it's his experience-driven pithiness that drives most of his engagement.

When I first met Ed in early 2017, he still had only a few thousand followers. We talked mostly about his experience going into boxing and then writing his own book. By the next year, he had ballooned to nearly 50,000 followers and finished a second book. He did this all while finishing his degree, training for boxing and competitive chess, taking paid speaking engagements, and doing both consulting and affiliate sales.

Because of his personal brand, Ed has more opportunities than he could have imagined just a few years earlier.

Ed is a good example of two notoriously difficult achievements in personal branding—both of which derive from *a lot* of real-world experience.

First, Ed's personal brand focuses on a large, competitive market—personal development. His unique positioning combines personal development with mathematics, physics, and boxing. All filtered through the lens of growing up in the ghetto.

Second, Ed built his brand largely through social media. He can do this because he (1) isn't attempting to put on some front that is incoherent with his story (i.e., he's sincere and *authentic* in his positioning); and (2) he doesn't let social media use him. Recall from Chapter 3 that social media companies have a strong incentive to build a positive feedback loop between you getting distracted and checking them. They employ hundreds of PhD cognitive scientists who are paid good money to distract you.

Most people *think* they can use social media to drive their personal brand but end up spending far more time than they plan *consuming* rather than creating on the platform.

Ed doesn't do this (Figure 4.6).

Ed Latimore
@EdLatimore
Following
Almost none.
Twitter is a drug. I'm the dealer, not the addict.
This is one of the not-so-minor reasons for my growth.
Aappo Ankelo @aappoja
Replying to @StartSellingSSS
how much do you actually spend time daily reading posts from the people you follow on Twitter? Always curious about this with popular and busy people. Same Q for @EdLatimore @AJA_Cortes @Nappyb0yy @naval @DamianProsa @IAmAdamRobinson
10:05 AM - 16 Oct 2018

FIGURE 4.6 twitter.com/edlatimore

Go to Ed's Twitter feed and you find a prolific rate of content creation. The rate is so high, you have to ask, "When does he have time to consume content?" He doesn't. He spends most of his time on the platform *creating* and putting out content.

Also note that Ed doesn't spread himself thin by trying to create content that works for every platform. He doubles down on what works. His preferred medium is Twitter, which he uses to drive traffic to his site, where he captures email addresses of the right people.

Few people can pull this off—my recommendation is to start on a specific value-driven positioning statement relating to your skills, unless you have a unique and unusual story you can tell eloquently through its own lens.

KEY TAKEAWAYS

- **Your personal brand is a signaling tool.** Use it to signal your experience, skills, knowledge, and positive traits to the right people. It's not an end in itself. Focus on creating a strong track record first. All sizzle and no steak is a negative signal.
- **Own your platform.** Build out your personal website and give the right people reason to stay in touch with you through an email list.
- **Drive the right people to your website** with Brand Builders that meet them where they already spend time online.

ACTION ITEMS

Beginner (You don't have a website yet.)

1. Go to www.namecheap.com and search for your name as a URL (e.g., zakslayback.com). Buy the .com domain. If it is not available, try variations on your name.
2. Download the Personal Website Checklist at zakslayback .com/book/pwchecklist.

Intermediate (You have a website, but you don't actively grow your own list.)

1. Install a lead capture on your website. Use Mailchimp, ConvertKit, or OptinMonster.
2. Based on what you know, brainstorm five different lead magnets you could create or install on the lead capture.
3. Download the *Personal Website Lead Magnet Guide* at zakslayback.com/book/leadmagnetguide.

Advanced (You have a website and a list, but you want to build your brand out.)

1. Build out your own Cabinet of Models for unleashing your personal brand. Who are the experts in your field? Whom can you work under? Whom can you hire? Whom can you meet with?
2. Build out a spreadsheet for your own Brand Builders. Include a tab for guest posts, a tab for podcasts, and a tab for vlogs that you can reach out to.
3. Download *12 Done-For-You Email Scripts* to get scripts to build out your Brand Builders: zakslayback.com/12-done-for -you-email-scripts-free.

CHAPTER

5

Connect

Build a World-Class Network Without Feeling Sleazy, Get Busy People to Talk to You, and Have Fun Doing It

It's never been easier to build a world-class network and connect with influential people. Anybody can do it, even if you hate "net-working" and even if you think you don't have any network at all.

There was once a time when the only way you could meet influential decision makers was through clubs, colleges, and cartels. This is the idea behind "The Old Boys' Club." If you didn't know one of The Old Boys or become one yourself, you were out of luck. If you didn't get an introduction from somebody in your fraternity, your company, your union, or your family, the best you could hope for was waiting outside of smoke-filled rooms and trying to meet people on the way out.

Today, things are (thankfully) very different. The world's never been more connected.

Everybody in the developed world has an email address. And anybody can email them—including you. A few cold emails and introductions can mean the difference between having so many new opportunities you have to fight them off and sitting at home blasting out résumés while resenting your job.

You can land a coffee meeting that changes the entire course of your career. *You* can meet with your role models, pitch your biggest prospects, land your dream job, and build a world-class network. And it all starts with sending a few emails.

You don't have to go to a fancy college, come from an established family, or sleazily ingratiate your way to a world-class network.

Building a world-class network doesn't look like networking. It looks like having the audacity to let people know you can add value for them. It looks like relationship-building. It looks like taking the few extra steps that anybody can take but so few do.

This chapter walks you through a proven system to identify whom you need to connect with, how you can reach them, and what to do so that they listen and build a relationship with you.

WHY "NETWORKING EVENTS" ALMOST ALWAYS WASTE YOUR TIME

Most people approach networking the wrong way.

The first thing they do is print business cards, google "networking events near me," and then head off to the local happy hour, freshly printed business cards in hand, expecting to rub shoulders with employers, CEOs, and busy people they can ask for new opportunities.

Then they get there and . . . nothing. Instead of meeting with the "Who's Who" of their city and industry, they meet life insurance salesmen, job hunters, and people who turn out for the free food.

You've probably done this yourself. I did when I got started in my career.

My job was to find, connect with, and pitch CEOs, founders, entrepreneurs, and investors on a radical idea—to hire people without degrees for jobs that required them. I went to networking events, happy hours, networking conferences, and everything I could find online. I followed all the gurus' advice to go to meetup.com and find interesting groups and hang out with them. I pinged the people I went to college with and the alumni network from my university.

With a few exceptions, this drove few valuable connections. Most of the networking events were full of people like myself—people trying to find decision makers and CEOs , but few of these people themselves.

I realized that all the people I had to connect with weren't at the events. They weren't going to spend their evenings at an event where people exchange business cards and hang around free cheap Merlot and light beer. They had better things to do.

Two fundamental concepts became clear to me over the coming years: the importance of understanding *vertical networking* and *opportunity cost.*

You're Going to the Top!

To get ahead in your career, you don't need to network with just *anybody.*

Just like with personal branding, having the *biggest* network doesn't mean you have *the best.* Your world-class network should have people who can help you land deals, get jobs, pick up new clients, or help you learn new in-demand skills. In other words, you want to network vertically, not horizontally.

Most people network horizontally (Figure 5.1). They meet people near their general experience and career status. They may meet other people in different companies, industries, fields, and interests. They may meet them at networking events or in college or grad school. But, with a few exceptions, their network is full of people just like them in terms of experience and career status.

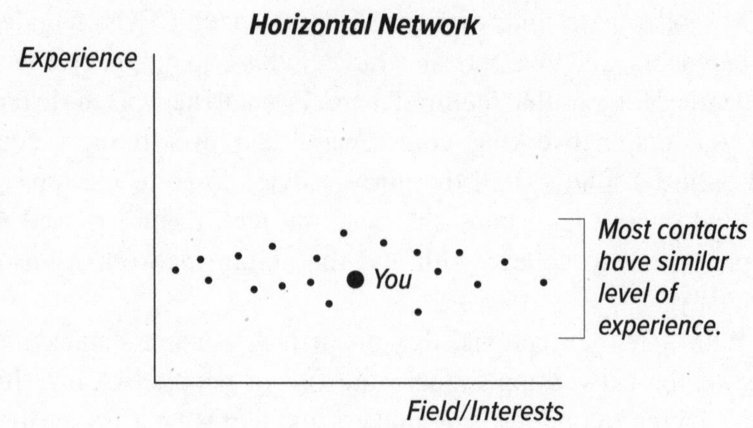

FIGURE 5.1 A horizontal network. Most of the people you know are around your age and experience.

This is a *horizontal network*. Horizontal networks look like the management consultant whose network consists of other management consultants and few senior VPs or CEOs who can promote them to a new project. Or the artist who knows a ton of other artists but few art critics or art brokers who can get her art out there. Or the coach who knows plenty of coaches but few executives who can bring her in to host a workshop. Or the job hunter who knows other people working junior jobs but few business owners who can hire him at the drop of a hat.

Horizontal networks are fine for social outings and having fun with people at your stage of life. But they rarely help with getting ahead in your career. Unless your college buddy refers you to his uncle who hires you, you're better off spending your time building a *vertical network* (Figure 5.2).

When doing business development, I realized that meeting with entry-level and junior employees mostly wasted my time. It'd take weeks to get a referral from them that actually ended up as a meeting with a decision maker. If I could land a meeting or a call with a senior executive, though, I could get a decision in days *and* end up meeting even more people through referral.

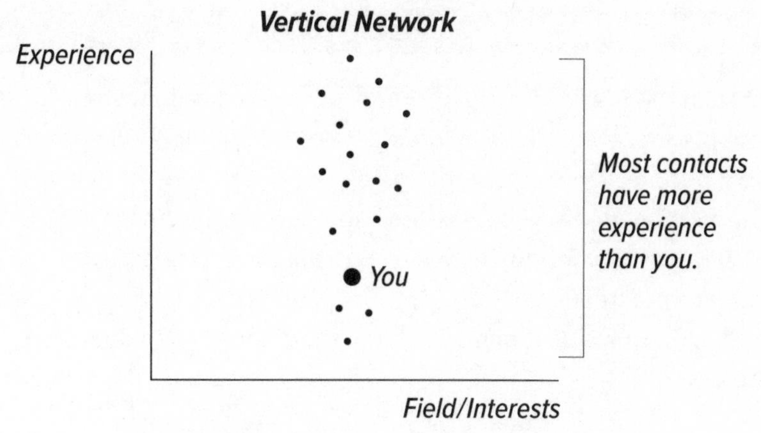

FIGURE 5.2 A vertical network. Most of the people you know are in different stages of their careers

What Savvy Founders Know That Novice Founders Miss

Startup founders raising money from venture capitalists run into this same problem. If they go through traditional channels when meeting with venture capital firms, they spend most of their time talking to junior employees called associates who are not investors. Associates are gatekeepers. Meeting with an associate usually means little more than just dropping off a business card.

Instead, savvy founders know to play the long game. They build relationships with investors, not junior employees, months in advance. When the time comes, they pitch the investor instead of going through the traditional process with the associates. The investor then refers them to *other* investors with similar (or even better) seniority and pull. This creates a snowball effect as the founder goes from knowing just a few investors to knowing upward of a dozen through a few introductions.

The *social proof* from the experienced investor makes it easier for other investors to come in. Savvy founders shave off *years* of one-on-one relationship-building and networking by building high-trust and quality relationships vertically with established investors.

"Steal" Established Trust

One of the reasons social proof works so well is that when people make decisions to work with other people—whether to hire people, to work together as business partners, or to invest in a company—they're constantly looking for reasons to say *no*. If they trust somebody else and that person trusts you, you can "steal" that trust.

"If Jon trusts Joe, and I trust Jon's judgment, then Joe must be OK."

You want to do the same for your career. Meet and build relationships with the people with a few key authorities:

- **Decision making.** They don't have to go through a whole bureaucratic structure to make decisions like hiring you, investing in your company, or working with you. When they do have to consult others, they actually have sway in the decision.
- **Social proof.** Other people take their opinions seriously. If others know that this person trusts you, they're more likely to trust you.
    - *Note:* This authority has a reversal. If you gain the trust of somebody with a *poor* reputation, this can hurt you. Lie down with dogs and you get fleas.
- **Referral power.** These people have *their own* valuable network to whom they can refer you. They can refer you *down* to subordinates (people take a referral from the boss seriously) or they can refer you *horizontally* to other experienced people.

To figure out where you meet these people, think of the opportunity cost to their decisions.

That Networking Event's Gonna Cost Something

Opportunity cost applies to more than just prioritizing your work (Chapters 2 and 3).

It applies to how you spend your leisure time, what you read, and with whom you hang out. If you spend an evening at a networking event, your opportunity cost is everything else you could have done that evening.

Think of the *kind* of people you want in your network. How much does their time cost? How old are they? Do they have a family? What does their average day look like? How do you think they want to spend their evenings?

Remember, most people only want to go to so many events in a month. So, you have to think about what kinds of events they *do* want to go to.

The right people for you to network with have valuable time. They're busy people. Their calendars are always full with others trying to meet with them.

They spend their time on the highest-value activities for themselves. This means they network with *other* high-value people (people just as or more successful than they are). Depending on their general success and preferences, they may spend their time in philanthropic events as a donor. They spend time at workshops improving their skills. When they're not at work events or high-value meetings, they spend their little remaining time with their families and in leisure activities. They spend time doing the things that career success *lets* them do—like leisure, sports, and other events that are participated in as an end in themselves.

They don't spend time hanging out at networking happy hours.

If you want to network with influential, decision-making Very Busy People (VBPs) like CEOs, investors, founders, and experienced executives, go where they are. Think of how they prioritize their time and go from there.

And for the love of all that is good, don't commit the Seven Deadly Sins of Networking.

THE SEVEN DEADLY SINS OF NETWORKING

Once you understand the importance of meeting people experienced enough to help you, the Seven Deadly Sins of Networking reveal themselves. Committing these sins takes time away from authentic relationship-building and distracts you from building the network you can take with you throughout your career.

1. Going to "Networking Events"

This one is so important that my blog readers know it as Slayback's Silver Rule of Networking: *If you want to build a world-class network, don't go to events whose primary advertised purpose is "networking."*

This *doesn't* mean don't go to events. Events whose *secondary* or *tertiary* purposes are networking might prove valuable. These might be fundraising and charity events, sports and recreation events, workshops and education events, industry-specific conferences, and purely leisure events. But for these events, networking is just an added benefit, not the main purpose.

The important takeaway of the First Deadly Sin of Networking is that you should always ask yourself, "What kind of people will be at this event? Is this the kind of people I want to meet, connect with, and build a relationship with? How would *they* like to spend their time away from work?"

2. Creating Merely Transactional Relationships

Part of what gives networking a negative reputation is the transactional approach most people take to it. They don't work on building their networks until they *need* to and then come off as desperate and needy at events.

Transactional relationships feel weird to people. They feel artificial and forced. If you approach networking with a mindset of, "What's in it for me?" instead of "What can I do to help this other person?" you'll come off as insincere and sleazy. People may take a meeting or do an introduction for somebody they meet transactionally, but they won't invest their own *social capital* in somebody they meet transactionally.

Think of a friend who only calls you when he needs something from you. If you never interact with him outside of the context of him making requests on you, you stop viewing him as a "friend." He becomes "yet another person who wants something from me."

This is every day in the life of a successful Very Busy Person. They constantly have people making asks of them and trying to get something out of them. Stand apart from the pack by taking a sincere interest in these people and their lives. View your "networking" activities as just getting your foot in the door. Any asks come later once you've built a relationship.

3. Seeking Status and Ignoring Those Who Aren't Flashy

Do not forget to show hospitality to strangers,
for by so doing some people have shown
hospitality to angels without knowing it.

—HEBREWS 13:2, NIV

When meeting new people, don't automatically gravitate toward the highest status person and ignore lower-status people. Take an active interest in everybody you meet, even those you don't know or don't expect to be interesting.

You want to do this for at least two reasons.

First, treating lower-status people poorly is a negative signal. You don't want to develop the reputation as a "star-lover"—somebody who only tries to build relationships with high-status people.

Second, you don't know whom you don't know. Somebody you expect to be low status or a complete stranger may actually be well-connected and interesting, if only you engaged with them.

Hebrews 13:2 says to show hospitality to strangers, because you don't know if you may be entertaining angels. This is doubly true for the world of relationship-building. Outside of some dysfunctional corporate environments, those who flaunt their status often fail to achieve high status. Some of the most helpful people you'll meet don't appear to be high status the first time you meet them.

4. Not Breaking Scripts

"What do you do?" is the networking equivalent of "So how about that weather?"

Don't ask it unless you want to kill the conversation.

People navigate social situations based on contextual "scripts." When you get asked certain questions, you know to answer with certain answers. Your eyes glaze over, and your mind goes into "conversational autopilot." Questions like, "Where did you go to school?" "What do you do?" "How long have you lived here?" "How do you know [host]?" all initiate conversational scripts. This makes talking to other people easier and less cognitively demanding.

It also makes the conversations less memorable.

When meeting people for the first time, focus on leaving a positive impression in their mind. When you follow up later and they see your name, they remember, "Oh! Yes! I do remember that person."

You don't make an impression by initiating scripts. You make an impression by asking questions that people *don't* expect.

The trick is making a *positive* impression. Anybody can ask unusual or unexpected questions. Doing so poorly looks creepy and weird. Doing so well looks creative and original. It signals that you're thinking relationally and not just transactionally. Do this by breaking scripts.

Breaking scripts means asking questions or making observations that pleasantly surprise people in conversation. You may ask them about a detail in the conversation or take notice of a detail in their outfit. You may do research on them beforehand and know to ask about a unique experience they had or a detail about their company.

The important effect of breaking scripts is that you don't allow conversations to go into autopilot. Don't let people's eyes glaze over. Notice details and ask yourself, "If I were this person, what would I *want* to talk about?"

5. Not Having a Social Hobby

Try to develop a social hobby if you don't have one already.

A social hobby gives you an excuse to meet with people one-on-one in a context or an environment outside of coffee or drinks. It turns networking and relationship-building into a consumption good—something people can do just because they enjoy it. There's a reason why most successful professionals play a sport like golf or tennis.

Your social hobby doesn't have to be expensive, it just needs to be something the type of person you need to and want to meet with also enjoys. If the type of person you want to meet with enjoys being outside and doesn't have to spend a lot of money to have a good time, hiking in small groups gives you an excuse to invite them out with you. If they would enjoy cooking, take up cooking classes. If they'd enjoy shooting, take lessons and join a rifle club. Giving somebody a reason to spend a few hours with you doesn't have to be complex—just have fun.

A young real estate investor told me one day about how he invited a successful property owner out to shoot skeet. "I got to spend several hours with him. I don't think that's something I would have been able to do if I had asked him to grab coffee. He probably would have said no to that. But we had a blast. We're going to do it again, and he's going to bring along some of his friends."

6. Not Following up Immediately with an Appropriate Message

Don't expect a Very Busy Person to follow up with you or remember you. You won't be high up their list of priorities unless you make yourself.

All you need to do is make a positive impression that gets your foot in the door. Once you do this—at an event, in an online interaction, wherever—follow up to solidify yourself in the person's mind for future outreach.

Your follow-up should happen within 48 hours *max.* Ideally you follow up within 24 hours. The context of meeting you remains fresh in their mind at this point. It should be status-relevant (you should use the correct level of formality based on the power dynamics), and it should give them a sign that you want to do more than just say hi.

Immediately after meeting the person, make a note to yourself about what you talked about during the conversation. Highlight or emphasize anything you can speak to that would stand out in the conversation. These are called Relationship Triggers.

Relationship Triggers are phrases, names, or subjects that a Very Busy Person *already thinks about.* This signals to them that you're not just spamming a ton of people. It jogs their memory and makes it easier for them to remember who you are.

Some common Relationship Triggers include:

- Mutual connections
- A topic you spoke about or overheard them talk about in a group
- Issues they've spoken or written publicly about

Using a Relationship Trigger tells this person, "I was listening, I'm not just spamming you, and I'm not looking to be ultra-transactional here."

For example, you both talked about the relationship between technological change and economic stagnation. You can follow up and send the person an article by Tyler Cowen about his Great Stagnation thesis and how it's changed since the 2008 financial crisis.

Your goal here is to stand out from the crowd of people this Very Busy Person meets every week. When you follow up with these people in the future or meet them again, they can search your name in their inbox and find your previous follow-up. This tells them that you're less likely to be a time-suck—somebody who just wants to waste time and only cares about themselves.

People don't give time to time-sucks. Preempt any concerns about being a time-suck by being respectful and conscientious in your follow-ups.

7. Pitching Too Much Too Soon

Networking is like dating.

Both are tools for *starting* relationships. You date to figure out whether or not somebody will make a good romantic partner. You network to figure out whether or not somebody will make a good professional contact.

Just like with dating, it's possible to move too quickly in networking.

You don't ask somebody to marry you on a second date. And you don't ask people to make an important introduction, become a cofounder, or invest in your company after meeting them twice.

People go out of their way and do favors for other people once others accrue *social capital* with them. It takes time and work to accrue social capital. You have to prove to people you won't make them look bad in front of people whose opinions they value. You have to prove to people you won't waste their time. You have to prove to them that you'll make them look *good*.

Social Capital

You have *social capital* in all of your relationships. Think of it like a bank account for relationships.

As you build a relationship with somebody, prove yourself trustworthy and competent, and show you aren't just transacting with somebody, you accrue social capital. If you make excessive asks, burn the other person by making them look bad, or renege on your obligations, you withdraw social capital.

Every ask you make has a social capital cost. Asking too often or for too much too soon overdraws your social capital.

When you get to zero or negative social capital, others won't oblige your asks and you have to do *more* work to prove yourself.

Be conscious of the social capital you hold in your professional relationships. Don't be afraid of making asks, but know that you have to build the relationship first before you can expect positive replies.

Oliver Cromwell told his army during the invasion of Ireland, "Trust in God and keep your powder dry." Trust in your relationships and keep your social capital intact until you need it.

IT'S NOT ABOUT WHO YOU KNOW— IT'S ABOUT WHO YOU KNOW WHO KNOWS WHO YOU NEED TO KNOW

Building a world-class network isn't about shaking hands with the most successful people in the world. It's not about going to events. It's not about schmoozing and not about forcing yourself to become an extrovert.

It's about knowing people who know who you need to know.

You want to know people who *want* to make introductions for you. Your network should work for you, even while you're not actively meeting new people or going to events and shaking hands. People you know should tell others, "Oh! I should introduce you to [your name]. S/he's exactly the kind of person you want to talk to."

Your network should send opportunities to you.

To do this, you need to build a Mindful Network.

A Mindful Network is both a vertical and a relational network (Table 5.1). A Mindful Network has experienced, seasoned Very Busy People in it. They work with you because they know you aren't merely looking to make a quick buck and leave. They want to pull you into and involve you in the relationships they already have.

	RELATIONAL	TRANSACTIONAL
VERTICAL NETWORK	**Mindful Network.** Very Busy People who appreciate the value you can bring them.	**Mindless Network.** You shake hands with lots of successful people, but never build relationships with them.
HORIZONTAL NETWORK	Friends and peers.	Purely professional relationships.

TABLE 5.1 Mindful Networking vs. Mindless Networking. Focus on networking with people at different stages of their careers and building real, sincere relationships with them.

Your Own Personal Salesforce—the Mindful Networking Plan

A Mindful Network helps you get referrals for jobs, land unadvertised opportunities, connect with people who are hard to meet, and close new clients.

For example, some of Silicon Valley's biggest and most famous venture capitalists purposely make it difficult to meet them. They believe the best investments and the best founders can and should be referred to them. Meeting them through traditional avenues rarely works. Having a Mindful Network gets founders the referrals they need to investors and gets investors the relationships they need to quality investments.

Building a Mindful Network is like hiring your own salesforce to go out into the world and listen for opportunities for you. You can't be everywhere at once, but you can influence dozens or hundreds of people to want to help you.

Build your Mindful Network by completing the following steps and making a Mindful Networking Plan (Table 5.2).

VBPS	VBP HONEYPOTS	SUPER-CONNECTORS	SUPER-CONNECTOR HONEYPOTS

TABLE 5.2 The Mindful Networking Plan. You'll work from left to right. Download your template at zakslayback.com/book/mnp.

Step 1: Identify the Very Busy People You Need to Meet

Most people mindlessly network. They go out and try to meet people just for the sake of meeting them or with transactional, short-term ends in mind. Before you build your Mindful Network and begin the referral process, start with your end in mind.

What kinds of people do you need to meet? Why? What can you offer them?

Who are the people who might seem unreachable now but would make a difference in your career if you could connect with them? Whom do you have to build a vertical network with in order to get the deals, projects, jobs, or opportunities you're looking for? Who are the decision makers you need to know?

If you struggle with identifying the exact kind of person you need to connect with, use this sentence stem:

> If I knew . . . I could . . .
>
> For example:
>
> > If I knew seed stage investors, I could pitch them on funding my startup.
> >
> > If I knew CEOs of quickly growing venture-backed software companies with fewer than 50 employees, I could land freelance consulting gigs.
> >
> > If I knew art critics, I could convince them to feature my art in their magazines.
> >
> > If I knew maintenance managers at growing HVAC companies, I could convince them to try the software that I sell.

Get as specific as possible in describing the *type* of person. Put positive constraints on who they are by getting specific about why you need to meet *them*.

Why do you need to network with these people? What value can you add to their lives? And, how? Why do you want that opportunity? Continue asking why until you get a granular picture of what you would do if you were connected with that kind of person.

Maybe you think you just need to connect with CEOs, but what you really want is to land freelance writing opportunities for high-growth tech companies. Meeting the CEOs of Fortune 500 companies or small businesses won't be as helpful. You really want to connect with "CEOs of high-growth startups."

When I run office hours at colleges, incubators, and accelerators for early stage startup founders looking to raise capital, we sometimes run through this exercise. They start out saying they want to meet with investors so that they can pitch them.

I ask them *why* they want to pitch the investors, followed by why they want the investment, and finish up with what they want to do with the investment.

Eventually, we work down to what their plans are for the company. *This* defines the *type* of investor they need to talk to. Some see themselves building out great businesses that serve million-dollar and hundred-million-dollar markets. They may earn their investors two, three, or even five times their investments. That's *great* for the founders and *might* be good for the investors.

Some investors, like casual angel investors, may only want a two-, three-, or five-times return on their investment because they only make a few small investments every year. Other investors, like venture capital firms and active angel investors, look for gargantuan returns like 20 times. They make so many investments every year and expect many of them to fail, so strong investments must be *strong*.

For those who see themselves building out $500 million, $750 million, or even billion-dollar companies someday, it makes more sense to build relationships with venture capital firms.

Too often early stage founders think they just need to get in front of "investors" without thinking about their end goal first.

Then they go to raise investment and find that many of the investors they spent months or years building relationships with don't do the kind of investment they're looking for.

Know *why* you want to connect with a VBP. Then figure out what type of VBP you need to connect with. Describe them in detail in your VBP column of the Mindful Networking Plan table (Table 5.3). If you already know people who fall into this category, write down their names.

VBPS	VBP HONEYPOTS	SUPER-CONNECTORS	SUPER-CONNECTOR HONEYPOTS
• Early stage investors who invest in technology companies with some traction. • John Smith • Smith Capital Ventures			

TABLE 5.3 Example Mindful Networking Plan for a startup founder trying to find potential investors.

Step 2: Where Do They Spend Their Time?

Once you have an idea of whom you need to meet with and what you can offer them, figure out where they already spend their time.

Develop a shortlist of potential "honeypots" based on the incentives these VBPs face and the problems they have.

Honeypots can be either events (physical honeypots) or publications (mental honeypots). Combining your Brand Builders with VBP honeypots lets you get in front of them through what they read, listen to, and watch.

Find several people who meet your VBP profile—people you know, follow, or research online. Search their name on Google with quotation marks around it. Note where these people's names pop up. What kinds of articles cite them? What kinds of events are they speaking at or attending?

Make specific note of *nonobvious* honeypots. These typically fall into the work, charitable, and leisure categories.

- **Work.** Do they speak at conferences? Are they on the public attendee list for any conferences? These rarely look like "networking" events. Instead, they usually involve education going deep into a subject matter or exclusive events for people in their professional position.
- **Charitable.** Are they on any foundation boards? Have they written or been cited in articles published by nonprofits? What about their local religious organizations? Do these organizations host conferences, fund-raisers, or events?
- **Leisure.** Do their names pop up for any sporting events? Do they play a sport on the side? Is their name on the public attendee list of anything like a wine-tasting event?

Even if the people whose names you google are not *specific* people you want to meet, note what you find. If *they* spend their time at these kinds of events, chances are other people like them do, too.

The information you find from this research doubles as useful hooks for when you do meet these VBPs.

Use Your Cabinet of Models

You don't have to guess at what kind of person or event to search. Ask your mentors how they spend their time. Ask them if they know VBPs like the ones you want to meet and how these VBPs might spend their time.

If you have a close relationship with somebody like the VBPs you want to meet, talk to them. Informed research is good but talking to your right people is better.

Research publications *positioned toward* your VBPs. If you want to meet with teachers, don't look for publications about teaching for a general audience. Look for publications for teachers.

When I talk with the founders I meet, they often talk about how difficult it is to connect with actual investors. If they go through contact forms on websites or go to "investment" events, they get stuck talking to associates. I ask them where the actual investors might spend their time, what publications they might read, and what activities they might spend their time in outside of work. One place to start is by looking at the "Venture Capital" category on online magazines like Medium. From there, search the names of the investors on the publication and find out where else they spend time when they aren't working.

Make note of everything you find in your Mindful Networking Plan table (Table 5.4). Even note events that you can't attend or think are a stretch. You'll use this information later.

Step 3: Who Connects with Them Already? Find the Super-Connectors

Some people spend time connecting and building relationships with VBPs. They get paid to network and cultivate fruitful long-term relationships with these people.

And they're more accessible than VBPs.

These are *super-connectors.* Super-connectors *have* to connect with busy and interesting people as a function of their jobs or hobbies. While most people spend most of their time building a skill set and learning—with networking as an afterthought—super-connectors make networking a priority and a skill.

Connect and build relationships with super-connectors. While they build out and develop their own network, you can spend most of your time learning and executing.

The kind of super-connector with whom you should build a relationship is a function of the kind of VBP with whom you want to build a relationship.

VBPS	VBP HONEYPOTS	SUPER-CONNECTORS	SUPER-CONNECTOR HONEYPOTS
• Early stage investors who invest in technology companies with some traction. • John Smith • Smith Capital Ventures	**Publications** • *Hacker Noon* (Medium) • Medium Venture Capital top writers **Work** • TechCrunch Disrupt • SXSW • *Specific issue* deep-dive events (e.g., events about the future of neural nets) **Charitable** • Mackinac Center board member **Leisure** • Great Oaks Country Club tennis championship		

TABLE 5.4 Example Mindful Networking Plan after brainstorming and researching VBP honeypots.

For example, if you want to connect with busy CEOs of high-growth software companies, you can spend your time building relationships with podcasters who feature interviews with CEOs of high-growth software companies.

Or, if you want to meet investors, connecting with the founders of investor-backed companies gives you a direct line to a network of investors.

Here are some common super-connectors:

- **Podcasters.** Check previous episodes to see if a podcaster interviews people like your target VBPs.
- **Nonprofit fundraisers and executives.** Nonprofit fundraisers—usually called "development" or "gift officers," as well as nonprofit presidents and CEOs—spend pretty much all of their time building relationships with VBPs. Some of these jobs require more than 80 percent of the time on the road networking and building relationships.
- **High-end salespeople.** The lifetime value of high-end customers can be hundreds of thousands or millions of dollars. High-end salespeople—who sell high-ticket luxury items or premium business products—spend much of their time cultivating and maintaining existing relationships.
- **Management consultants.** While management consultants don't spend most of their time networking, they do spend most of the time on the road. This lets them build large networks across multiple cities in a few short years.
- **PR professionals.** If you want to build relationships with journalists and media contacts, start by building relationships with PR professionals who have already spent years building media lists.
- **Startup founders.** While these may be VBPs of their own type, if you're also a startup founder, other founders can provide contacts for investors, advisors, and partners.

Find super-connectors for your specific VBPs by looking both for media appearances by the VBP (e.g., podcast interviews or blogger interviews) and for people who *work for* or *have an incentive to be connected with* the VBP.

For example, if you want to connect with high-net-worth individuals in your city, your research should show you that the board members of most (smaller) nonprofits are major donors to those nonprofits.

Find several nonprofits whose missions you like, confirm that their board members look like the VBPs with whom you want to connect, and research their development staff. If you target nonprofits with which you don't actually enjoy working, you'll lose interest or appear obviously transactional before building a proper relationship with the super-connectors.

The startup founders I talk to work on finding super-connectors related to the VBP honeypots for startup investors. These might be nonprofit fundraisers for organizations investors donate, podcasters who interview these investors, or other founders who've raised capital themselves (Table 5.5).

VBPS	VBP HONEYPOTS	SUPER-CONNECTORS	SUPER-CONNECTOR HONEYPOTS
• Early stage investors who invest in technology companies with some traction. • John Smith • Smith Capital Ventures	**Publications** • *Hacker Noon* (Medium) • Medium Venture Capital top writers **Work** • TechCrunch Disrupt • SXSW • *Specific issue* deep-dive events (e.g., events about the future of neural nets) **Charitable** • Mackinac Center board member **Leisure** • Great Oaks Country Club tennis championship	• Mackinac Center development staff • Gifts Officer • President • Great Oaks Country Club tennis coaches • Podcasters who interviewed John Smith and his peers • Work event organizers	

TABLE 5.5 Example super-connectors who might be around potential investors.

Step 4: Where Do the Super-Connectors Spend Their Time?

Meet the super-connectors where they already spend their time.

Most super-connectors have fewer inbound requests to meet than VBPs. If you can catch their attention, it's easier to land a meeting with them and build a relationship than by going directly to a VBP.

Just like VBPs, super-connectors spend their time at work, charitable, and leisure events. Use the same research process you used to find out VBP honeypots to find out super-connector honeypots (Table 5.6).

For example, if you want to meet with a prolific podcaster whose guests you admire, go through previous episodes to see if he regularly attends a specific kind of conference or event. Even if you find little in terms of events, you'll find Relationship Triggers you can use to craft a cold email to him and start a conversation.

The founders I meet with go through this process and realize that they already know super-connectors and super-connector honeypots. It turns out that the pitch days they attend, the conferences they sit in on, and the publications they read all have super-connectors at them.

Step 5: Reach Out to Super-Connectors

Build relationships with super-connectors.

There are three easy ways to connect with super-connectors:

1. Introductions from people you already know
2. Meet them at honeypot events
3. Send cold emails

Introductions from People You Already Know

Warm introductions from your existing network always have the highest chances of working. You don't need a massive vertical network to connect with and meet super-connectors. You just need to know a few people who know a few people. And you already

VBPS	VBP HONEYPOTS	SUPER-CONNECTORS	SUPER-CONNECTOR HONEYPOTS
• Early stage investors who invest in technology companies with some traction. • John Smith • Smith Capital Ventures	**Publications** • *Hacker Noon* (Medium) • Medium Venture Capital top writers **Work** • TechCrunch Disrupt • SXSW • *Specific issue* deep-dive events (e.g., events about the future of neural nets) **Charitable** • Mackinac Center board member **Leisure** • Great Oaks Country Club tennis championship	• Mackinac Center development staff • Gifts Officer • President • Great Oaks Country Club tennis coaches • Podcasters who interviewed John Smith and his peers • Work event organizers	• Founder socials in the Bay Area • Guest lectures at the local university by exited founders • Demo days at the local accelerators • Podcaster conferences • *Hacker Noon*

TABLE 5.6 The full Mindful Networking Plan for an example startup founder trying to find early stage investors.

know these people through your Cabinet of Models and your personal brand.

Before asking for introductions to super-connectors, get a clear vision of *the exact super-connector* or *type of super-connector* you can meet. Be as specific as possible so that when you send your introduction request to your existing network, people can immediately connect you to the right person.

Open-ended requests are actually harder for people to answer than pointed requests. If you ask people for introductions generally, they usually will either connect you with somebody who may not be the kind of person you should meet, or they tell you they can't think of anybody.

Don't put the burden on others to know

Make making introductions *easy* for people.

What does your super-connector look like? What do they do? Where do they work? How old are they? Where do they live? Why do you want to meet with them? Where did you hear about them?

If you have a specific person in mind, ask for an introduction to that person. If you don't, give as many parameters as possible.

Here's an email script you can use to request an introduction:

> Hi ***[First name]***,
>
> I'm looking to learn more about ***[sector, industry, whatever your target super-connector works in]*** because ***[why you want to learn more]***. I know you're well-connected, and I was wondering if you'd be open to introducing me to two people who ***[your descriptors of the super-connectors]***.
>
> I'd like to ***[what you want to do with the super-connectors—you can use your personal website as a piece of collateral here]***.
>
> Would you be open to this? If so, I can pass along a blurb about myself that you can forward.
>
> Thanks!
>
> ***[Your name]***

Give people context. This helps them figure out what kind of person to introduce you to.

Two people is a discrete number that immediately prompts the reader to think of people they can introduce you to. Don't leave the number open-ended.

Tell them exactly the kind of person you want to meet.

Let them know why you want the introduction. This reduces the risk of making the introduction and assures them you won't make them look bad.

This also reduces the risk of saying yes. You're letting them know you'll make it as easy as "copy, paste, forward" to do the intro.

Use "Thanks" for casual or close connections, use "thank you" for formal or distant connections.

Here's what that might look like for somebody who wants to be connected with important decision makers who have to negotiate big deals:

> Hi Scot,
>
> I'm looking to learn more about negotiating—particularly about high-ticket negotiating and high-stakes political negotiating. As I'm getting more experience in this space, I realize this is something I really need to improve.
>
> I know you're well-connected to people doing complex sales and negotiating. I was wondering if you'd be open to introducing me to two negotiating consultants with 10+ years of experience whom you know.
>
> I'd like to interview them for my blog and learn more about how they got where they are.
>
> Would you be open to this? If so, I can pass along a forwardable blurb you can use.
>
> Thanks!

If you have specific people in mind whom you *know* the contact you're emailing knows, you can name them instead of asking for two contacts who meet the parameters you outline.

Have a prepared blurb about yourself to send along as soon as your contact says yes to doing an introduction. The blurb can either be in the first person or the third person, and it should outline why you are relevant to the person you want an introduction to.

When requesting introductions, be aware of both the social capital you have with your contact and of the power dynamics of introductions.

If you ask three people from your current network—like your advisors and mentors in your Cabinet of Models—for two introductions each and they say yes, you've immediately added six super-connectors to your network with just a few emails.

Meet Them at Honeypot Events

Meeting super-connectors at honeypot events gives you face time with them and an urgent reason to follow up.

Before attending an event, get an idea of the super-connectors attending and how you might find them. If they work for a sponsoring organization, for example, find the organization's table and ask to meet them. If they're an organizer of the event, ask to meet them when checking in.

When meeting, speak to them at least long enough to learn about them and to make a positive impression on them. Make yourself stick out from the torrent of follow-up emails by mentioning a memorable element about the conversation—even if it is that you liked what they were wearing or had to say at a talk.

Should you have the opportunity to sit down and start building a relationship with them at the event (e.g., you grab coffee the next day and have a great conversation), ask them for the names of two people you should meet *at the event*. If you can't do this, don't worry. You'll do this after following up with them.

After meeting at the event, send a follow-up email. The follow-up email just needs to remind them of who you are and get them to reply.

Actionable Follow-Ups vs. Nonactionable Follow-Ups

In some cases, it makes sense to send a follow-up email that doesn't include an ask for a phone call or meeting. Send these kinds of follow-ups to VBPs or in general networking contexts.

When meeting super-connectors, use the follow-up to start building a relationship with them. Unless you had the opportunity to sit down together when you met them, include a request for a meeting, call, or at least some kind of email–based exchange in your follow-up.

For example, if you meet a super-connector at an event and chat briefly about the importance of standing out in doing marketing, send a follow-up like this:

> Hi John,
>
> It was a pleasure meeting you at Railvolution last week. I really enjoyed chatting with you about standing out in doing traditional PR.
>
> Not sure if you've read it, but Ryan Holiday's book *Trust Me, I'm Lying* is great on this topic. I thought you might enjoy this post of his on "lazy PR"—ryanholiday .net/the-epitome-of-lazy-pr/.
>
> *The Ryan Holiday article isn't an ask—it's a Relationship Trigger. It's used to remind the reader about the conversation that prompted the follow-up email.*
>
> I'm actually going to be out in San Francisco next week and would love to grab a cup of coffee with you near your office Thursday or Friday morning. Would you be open to that? I'll send along a few times, if so.

The email ends with a request to grab coffee. Since the emailer already met John, this isn't too strong an ask. Even if John declines, it lets him know, "I'm interested in continuing this conversation."

Send Cold Emails

Sending cold emails is an underutilized networking tool. While cold emails have a lower reply rate than warm introductions, they should be used by anybody serious about growing a Mindful Network.

Sending successful cold emails comes down to making sure your email doesn't look like spam and is clear and compelling in what you want. Whether cold emailing VBPs or super-connectors, you don't want readers to think you're sending the same email to dozens or hundreds of people. That's the difference between a cold email and spam.

Before sending a cold email, find a *reason* to reach out to the person. Look for something that people will recognize or with which they'll identify. This might be a podcast episode, an article, or some other media the super-connector created or was featured in. Actually consume the media—there's nothing worse than receiving an email where somebody says she listened to an interview with you but it is obvious she didn't.

Look up people's contact info using a tool like FindThatLead or Hunter.

Write them an email that answers these questions, in this order:

1. Who are you?
2. Do I know you?
3. How did you get my info, and why are you emailing me?
4. What do you want?
5. If you are making any claims, how can you prove them?
6. What *specific* action do you want me to take?

Use a subject line that makes your intent in the email and your point of reference clear. Subject lines like, "per your recent article" or "[mutual contact] told me to email you" work well.

Here's what a cold email to a super-connector who is a local podcaster might look like:

> **Subject Line:** Just moved to Cincinnati, love your podcast
>
> Chris,
>
> My name is Fred Tunny. You don't know me, but I just moved to Cincinnati from New York and have been getting my bearings in the city. I've been looking for local podcasters who know about sales—I've been in sales for the last five years, myself—and I came across your show. I really enjoyed episode 36 with Oren Klaff—*Pitch Anything* is one of my go-to books and I was shocked to hear

This shows the reader that Fred actually listened to the podcast episode he references.

it took him so long to write it. I actually wrote an article comparing *Pitch Anything* to *SPIN Selling*: ***[LINK]***.

> *Use your personal website and personal brand as networking collateral. This shows the reader that the sender actually has an established interest in sales.*

I know you're a busy guy, but I'd love to grab a drink and learn more about how you got into podcasting about sales sometime in the next few weeks.

> *While not super-focused, this lets the reader know that the sender has a specific reason for reaching out.*

Would you be open to this? I'll send along some dates, if so.

Thanks,

Fred

Use your personal brand as collateral. If you've also written, spoken, or created content on a subject related to the super-connector, share that. That alone can provide a mutual point of rapport that signals to super-connectors that you might not waste their time.

Avoid abstract questions and multiple calls to action. Phrases like, "I'd like to pick your brain," and "let me know what you think" lack focus and signal to readers that you may waste their time. Pointed, singular questions with a clear purpose signal that you might be worth hopping on the phone with or meeting in person.

Acknowledge ignorance. People are surprisingly open to helping others when you approach them honestly and sincerely. If you're just starting your career or making a big transition, let recipients know that. Tell them why you want to speak to *them* in particular. Content creators in particular (e.g., podcasters, writers, editors) appreciate acknowledgment for their work. Don't be ingratiating, but don't be needlessly formal and cold.

While cold emailing doesn't work as well as getting warm introductions or meeting people face-to-face, it's relatively easy to do and highly scalable. You can send a few cold emails every week for essentially zero cost and land one or two new meetings with super-connectors.

Don't Be a Jerk

Don't forget the Second Deadly Sin of Networking. You're *building a relationship* with super-connectors. Don't treat them as a mere means to an end so that you can meet with the VBPs they know.

Most super-connectors guard their relationships with VBPs. They know that one or two poor introductions make them look bad and make it harder to meet with the VBP down the line. Reach out to people with whom you actually want to be friends. This caps your downside—you get a friendship out of the relationship in the worst-case scenario—and makes the process enjoyable.

Step 6: Activate Your Super-Connectors: Make It Clear Those You Want to Meet

You shouldn't expect super-connectors to make introductions for you unless that's something you specifically asked for. This doesn't have to be awkward. Most people don't know how to "activate" their connections and let them know, "Hey, send people my way."

Take the awkwardness out of introductions through focusing on passive and active referrals.

Passive Referrals (Content-Driven)

Passive referrals happen when super-connectors have a light bulb moment and realize that you need to meet a VBP they know. Get passive referrals by staying *front-of-mind* for a specific niche and letting your super-connectors know that you want to meet a specific type of VBP.

Use your personal website to stay front-of-mind in your positioning. Make a point to feature interviews with the kinds of VBPs you'd like to meet. If you want to meet art critics, for example, occasionally make a point to publish an interview with an art critic on your website.

Send this content to super-connectors when you want to activate them. Tell them you're interested in producing more content like this and you'd like for them to connect you to one or two VBPs you can interview. After they do the introduction, let them know you'll take any other introductions in the future. Offer to do the same for them.

WIIFM—Super-Connectors

If you're asking for introductions for business purposes—to land new clients or close deals—offer referral fees to your super-connectors, even if your company doesn't have a referral program.

If there isn't a direct financial payoff to your networking, directly ask your super-connectors what you can do for them. When cashing in on others' social capital, use it as an opportunity to build your own.

Ask super-connectors if you can add them to your email list. Tell them they'll get emails from you when you have new content that relates to the introduction they made. Most will say yes. This helps you stay front-of-mind for your super-connectors and increases the likelihood that they will send introductions your way.

Active Referrals

Use active referrals when you need to grow your network with a specific end in mind. Passive referrals add VBPs to your network whom you may call on some day with a pitch. Active referrals add VBPs to your network when you know exactly what you want to pitch. Use active referrals to get introductions to high-value VBPs whom your super-connectors might not otherwise introduce to you.

To figure out whether or not you should request an active referral, use this sentence stem:

If I met . . . I would pitch/ask/request ________________.

If you can't confidently and clearly answer that question, hold off on making active referral requests. Few things hurt your chances more than asking for an introduction "just because." When you *can* confidently answer that question, reach out to your super-connector.

Follow the same rules you followed in Step 5.

HOW TO BUILD A WORLD-CLASS NETWORK, EVEN IF YOU HAVE NO IDEA WHERE TO START . . . (PART 1)

I worked with AJ (AJGoldstein.com) when he launched his data science consulting business in 2017. In a few short months, AJ's business grew to tens of thousands in monthly recurring revenue and a team of five data scientists. We worked together on business development, productivity, networking, and strategy for AJ's career.

This was his positioning:

> I help app-based wellness and mindfulness companies increase engagement and revenue by reducing user churn. I do this through analyzing drop-off point data and making recommendations on improving user on-boarding.

Besides a summer internship at a prominent meditation app company, AJ entered this field with no real network. He tried networking events and meetup.com to no avail—most of the attendees were more interested in talking about data conceptually rather than how it can actually be used in companies.

He turned his attention to meeting super-connectors through attending industry conferences, cold emailing leading data scientists in his field, and becoming a super-connector himself. He launched a data science podcast (*Data Journeys*) and used that as a hook for reaching out to prominent data scientists.

AJ made a point to ask people at the end of calls if they knew other people he should talk to. When they told him they did, he offered to send along a forwardable blurb.

This forwardable blurb helped in two ways:

1. **It made it *ridiculously easy* for the super-connector to make an introduction.** One of the biggest reasons introductions don't happen (even after people say they will) is that it's hard to do them. The person requesting the introduction puts the burden of describing *them* on the person *making* the introduction. This is cognitively taxing and takes time. Forwardable blurbs make introductions as easy as clicking "Forward" in the email client and take the burden off the person making the introduction.
2. **It made it *obvious* what he wanted.** AJ's blurbs painted a clear and compelling picture of why somebody should speak to him. They weren't just copy-and-pasted from an About page or a biography. He tailored each blurb for the specific person he wanted to meet. The blurb made his positioning clear and answered the question, "What's in it for me?" for the reader. This put his readers in a position of "Why *not* speak to him?"

In less than 10 months, AJ became one of the best-connected people in the small-but-growing mindfulness space. He actually found himself getting requests from companies *outside* his area of expertise because his positioning as a data scientist working with mindfulness companies was so strong.

AJ's dream client was Oak Meditation, led by one of the biggest superstars in the mindfulness space—Kevin Rose. A big Tim Ferriss fan, AJ loved Kevin's approach to meditation and mindfulness and knew that he had something to offer him if he could land an introduction.

On June 11, 2018, AJ sent a forwardable blurb to a mutual connection. He asked for an introduction to Kevin Rose.

Five hours later, he got a reply:

> I'd love to chat!
>
> Kevin

Through concerted networking and building a Mindful Networking Plan, AJ landed his dream-meeting with a superstar. He used that to open up opportunities he could only have dreamed of just a few weeks later. See Part 2 in Chapter 6 for how he pitched himself and closed those dream opportunities.

KEY TAKEAWAYS

- **Networking** is about building social capital and proving to other people that you won't waste time, won't make them look bad, and are trustworthy.
- **Don't be transactional.**
- **Know who you want to meet and why.** Understand opportunity cost and the incentives that Very Busy People face when choosing how to spend their time.
- **Build relationships** with people who have already built relationships with Very Busy People you want to meet.
- **Be accessible** and make it easy for people to refer others to you.
- **Be mindful of others' time**—don't network mindlessly.

ACTION ITEMS

1. Download your own Mindful Networking Plan table at zakslayback.com/book/mnp.
2. Build your own Mindful Networking Plan using the steps above and an MNP table.
3. Connect with at least two super-connectors in the next week.

CHAPTER

6

Close

Build Your Unfair Advantages, Confidently Pitch Yourself, and Make It Impossible for Others to Tell You No

Always be on the lookout for new opportunities.

Your personal brand does most of the work for you. Strong positioning tells others what you do and how you do it. Your brand signals your positive traits and disqualifies most people you don't want to work with. Your Mindful Networking Plan brings in new connections to help you make new opportunities a reality.

But whether you want to make a major career transition, grow your business, or just get a promotion, you need to actually *close* the opportunities that come to you.

This chapter walks you through which opportunities to pursue and which to ignore. You'll learn how to approach new opportunities so that even if they don't work out, you end up in a better place than if you didn't pursue them in the first place. You'll finally learn how to make important decision makers fight each other for the chance to work with you—even if you think that sounds silly right now.

You are a salesperson—whether you like it or not.

In the 1992 classic film *Glengarry Glen Ross*, Alec Baldwin gives a vulgar motivational speech to a room full of salesmen. The message is clear: "A–B–C. Always. Be. Closing."

Early nineties corporate bravado aside, the advice carries to more than just sales. Even if you've never completed a sale in your life and the idea of Alec Baldwin imploring you to close new leads while swearing at you turns your stomach, you are a salesperson.

You're a salesperson for the valuable brand of *you*.

What would it feel like to get a job offer that pays you twice what you earn now? Or to have so many client opportunities that you have to turn people down? Maybe have the chance to lead a new team? Perhaps have your investor round be oversubscribed?

What Does "Closing" Mean to You?

"Closing new leads" doesn't mean the same thing for every career. If you work a nine-to-five job and enjoy doing so, closing new leads might mean interviewing for new jobs. If you run a freelance consulting business, closing new leads might mean tracking down new consulting clients. If you're an intellectual or an academic, closing new leads might mean applying for a fellowship or grant, even while you work in a role you enjoy.

WHY YOU SHOULD BE CLOSING (EVEN IF YOU'RE HAPPY WITH WHAT YOU HAVE NOW)

Most people only pursue new opportunities when they *have* to. They get unhappy with their job and decide to look for a new one.

They lose a client and decide they need to start prospecting again. They put off courting investors until they really need the money.

But this puts them at a disadvantage.

Incorporating a closer's philosophy to your career gives you at least three distinct unfair advantages in landing opportunities:

1. Negotiating and confidence
2. Skills
3. Self-awareness

Negotiation and Confidence

If you were negotiating with somebody you wanted to hire and you knew they could walk, would you be more or less likely to offer them a better deal to work with you?

What if you were an investor and you wanted to invest in a company?

Or an art journalist who wanted to exclusively cover a new and upcoming artist?

Or even just a manager who had a great employee you wanted to keep around?

Closing new opportunities, even when you're happy with your current ones, gives you what William Ury, author of *Getting to Yes* and *Getting Past No*, calls a Best Alternative to a Negotiated Agreement (BATNA).

You're not only more confident asking for more but also less likely to be pushed around in negotiations when you have other options. And if those on the other side know they can find plenty of other options to replace you, they'll treat you with a "take it or leave it" approach.

In any negotiation, the party that cares less wins.

This is one of the reasons why you should at least *research* what your peers earn when negotiating a deal, a raise, or an investment. If you know you can get a great deal elsewhere, you're less likely to undernegotiate and more likely to call out the other side when they lowball your offer.

You gain confidence that pays off by the end of the negotiations.

It's one thing to say feel-good affirmations and read self-help. It's another to see your other options in front of you in cold ink and paper.

An old college friend grabbed lunch with me on a work trip to Pittsburgh. He worked what many at our school considered a dream job—he was a consultant at *the* top-tier management consulting firm in the world. And he was miserable.

He felt trapped. Every week was the same. Same kinds of assignments. Same kinds of trips. Same kinds of work. But he wasn't sure if he wanted to quit. He made good money. The job wasn't *awful.*

"You need a BATNA," I told him.

"A what?"

"Go interview for jobs elsewhere. Even if you don't plan on quitting, you'll gain the confidence to ask your boss to move you to new projects. You'll have an out. You can quit if you want. But I would bet you that your boss would actually appreciate knowing his subordinates are in demand. Just don't do it on company time and you're golden."

A month later, he interviewed for chief of staff jobs at a few startups and a new business development role at SpaceX.

"You gonna take it?" He was psyched about the SpaceX opportunity.

"Maybe. I'm not sure. It seems amazing. At least I feel great about my time here now, though. I finally feel like I can focus on work knowing I can leave at any time I want. I don't feel trapped anymore." He ended up not taking the opportunity but instead got a huge raise at work. Because he knew he could explore outside options, he no longer felt trapped. Closing gave him options, even if he didn't take those options.

Skills

Closing is a skill.

Whether interviewing for a job, pitching investors, closing clients, or just convincing somebody to buy into your project, practice the skill of pitching if you want to get better at pitching. You can read as many books on interviewing, pitching, or talking to others as you want, but ultimately much of pitching success comes down to tacit knowing, reflexively, in the moment, what to say and do.

By taking a closer's approach to your career, you keep your self-pitching skills sharp. When you *really* want to land that new opportunity, you don't have to stress over interviewing or pitching. You've practiced. You know what to do.

Self-pitching comes down to more than just interviewing, too. Industry standards and expectations change. What passed as an intense vetting process years ago becomes the norm. This applies doubly if you work in any technical field, with technical interviews or reviews.

As you get older and more experienced, the payoff from strong self-pitching skills increases relative to your peer group. While your peers allow their self-pitching skills to atrophy, expecting just to get by on their experience, you set yourself apart. Few experienced professionals have both the experience needed to succeed and the ability to convey that well to others.

Self-Awareness

You don't know what you don't know about yourself and the market.

One of the best ways to get constructive feedback on what skills to improve and develop is to regularly go for new opportunities. What passes as skilled and experienced in one company may not pass as the same in another company. What passes as a "full-stack" skill set in one city may not pass as the same in another city.

There are two ways to gain self-awareness and improve your skills.

You could take a top-down approach and research online. Then you could set out to develop those skills and *hope* you aren't spending your time developing the wrong skills. You could *hope* how you're developing the skills is a contemporary approach in your industry. And you could *hope* that how you choose to signal those skills makes sense for what you want to do.

Or you could take a bottom-up approach. Pitch yourself for new opportunities early and often. Along the way, get feedback on what to improve to increase your chances. Learn from potential mentors what you did wrong and what you can do better. You learn what, *exactly*, you need to do to build out the experience, portfolio, and signals in order to land the opportunity.

A young freelance software developer I mentored wanted to earn more money. Self-educated with an impressive portfolio for his age, he figured he stood a great chance of landing any opportunity. He applied for a full-stack software developer job at a company where he had a referral. He ended up getting rejected. He still lacked important skills. When he got feedback from the team, he asked what, exactly, he could do to get better as a developer. Not only did they tell him what they wanted to see next time he applied, they gave him book recommendations and told him about the tacit knowledge in their industry.

He knew what he needed to do to successfully land new opportunities going forward—and he had a new advisor in his Cabinet of Models.

We don't like to feel like failures. Most people find reasons not to take a closer's approach to their career that come back to a fear of failure. Interviewing for a great opportunity or pitching yourself to dream investors and getting told "no thanks" hurts. But the choice here isn't between failure and success. It's between potential failure when the stakes are low—and you have time to incorporate feedback—and failure when the stakes are high—and it's too late to incorporate feedback.

It's better to be proactively learning and risk minor failures than be reactive and risk major failures.

WHICH OPPORTUNITIES TO CLOSE (AND WHICH TO IGNORE)

As you build out your skills, your personal brand, and your network, the problem won't be finding opportunities. You'll have *too many* opportunities available. Learn which to ignore and which to pursue.

Say Yes to Asymmetric Opportunities

Pursue *asymmetric opportunities* (Figure 6.1).

Asymmetric opportunities cost little to pursue and give high reward if you succeed. Some examples of asymmetric opportunities are starting a side business that you can work on outside of the nine-to-five, taking job interviews that aren't time consuming, or pitching yourself to give a paid speech at a conference.

In each of these cases, the risk in failing is relatively low. Your side business isn't your main source of income. These job interviews don't require you to drop everything to pursue them. You don't make your main source of income as a paid speaker.

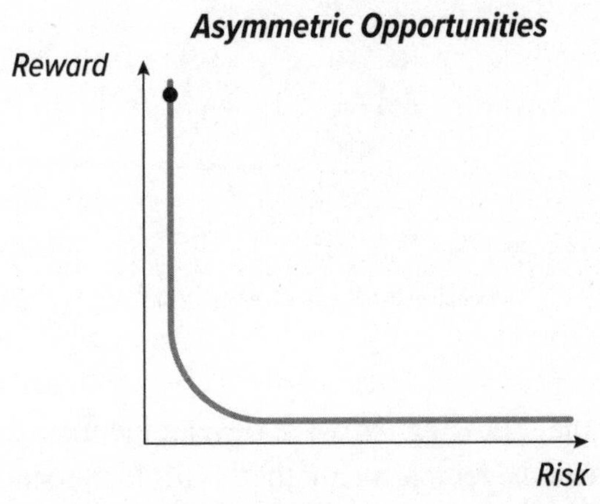

FIGURE 6.1 Asymmetric opportunities have little risk and high reward.

The payoff from success outweighs the risk of failure. That side business could eventually overtake your main source of income. Those job interviews could land you your dream job or networking opportunities with important decision makers at the company. Becoming a paid speaker means you can earn hundreds—or even thousands—of dollars per hour for your work.

Don't Forget the Intangible Rewards

Weigh the risk and rewards of any opportunity. Rewards often go beyond mere money and include intangibles like your talent stack, acquiring signals, and growing your network.

Building the Talent Stack

Dilbert creator Scott Adams popularized the *talent stack* in his book *How to Fail at Almost Everything and Still Win Big.* Your talent stack is the unique combination of skills you have that set you apart from your peers. A strong talent stack includes skills that allow you to serve your target audience better than your peers and in a unique way (Figure 6.2).

FIGURE 6.2 When you focus on one skill, you compete on whether or not you're the best *at that skill.*

For example, knowing software development is one skill. Mastering project management is another skill. Understanding how to influence and persuade others is yet another skill. Each of these skills unto itself opens up new opportunities. Combining these skills sets the skill-holder apart from her peers so that others *have no choice* but to go to her (Figures 6.3 through 6.5). A software developer who manages projects and persuades stakeholders well easily rises to leadership positions through talent stacking.

FIGURE 6.3 When you focus on two skills, you set yourself apart from the people focusing only on one skill.

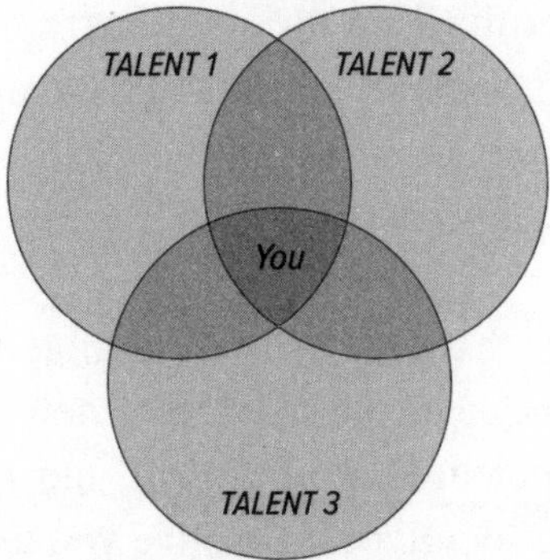

FIGURE 6.4 When you focus on three complementary skills, you further set yourself apart.

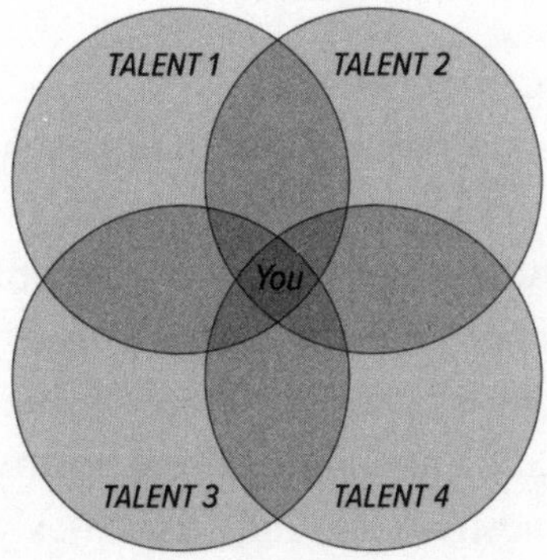

FIGURE 6.5 When you combine four complementary skills, you're uniquely set apart from your peers.

As you advance in your career, focus on building out a talent stack that gives you an unfair advantage relative to your peers. Don't *just* focus on opportunities that let you focus on your main skills. Instead of imitating your competition, pursue opportunities that allow you to sit at the unique intersection of several skills rarely found together.

Acquiring Stronger Signals

Pursue new opportunities that help you acquire and reinforce new signals.

As you advance in your career, you need new signals to lend credibility to your evolved positioning. Reframing new opportunities as unique signals helps you evolve and expand your positioning.

When considering an opportunity, ask yourself, "What *evidence* can I take away from this opportunity to reinforce what I want to signal?"

Any opportunity that results in a tangible product, service, or evidence of your work can be used as a new signal. Team-based projects present opportunities to collect and expand testimonials and endorsements. In-depth projects give you the chance to develop detailed success stories, useful for persuasion-heavy negotiations like getting hired or landing big clients.

Focus on what evidence you can create from new opportunities and what that evidence tells the right people about you.

Strategically Growing Your Network

Pursuing opportunities gives you a unique chance to grow your network.

Sometimes you don't have the *in* to meet big players or potential advisors or mentors unless you have something unique to offer them. Pursuing an opportunity with a Very Busy Person is a quick way to develop social capital and make a positive impression. Even if the opportunity doesn't work out, so long as you make a point of *doing a great job* and *not looking like an idiot*, you can earn a connection to call on for months or years down the line.

Don't Be an Idiot

Networking is a *secondary* benefit of taking opportunities. Don't *just* pursue opportunities because they might grow your network. That looks transactional and makes you look like a jerk.

Risk Is Often Lower Than You Think

We're hardwired to underestimate reward and overestimate risk.

Most risky decisions come down to losing two things: options and time. When weighing risks , ask yourself two questions, "Can I reverse this decision if I don't like it?" and "What else could I do with my time rather than pursuing this opportunity?"

Reversibility—Flip the Burden of Proof

Nobody wants to pursue a big opportunity only to regret it later. You don't want to quit your job for a job that turns out to be worse. You don't want to take investor money and learn that the investor is awful. You don't want to start a side business just to be saddled with extra responsibility and little to gain.

The reality is that most decisions are actually reversible—even big decisions like dropping out of college, quitting your job, or starting a business—and have a smaller long-term impact than we estimate at first.

Instead of getting caught up in "what if . . ." scenarios, flip the burden of proof and ask, "Why not do this?" Answer that question by interviewing others who made that choice, reaching out to them as advisors. "Why not launch a side business?" "Why not pitch myself as a paid speaker?" "Why not interview for that new job?"

Beware Confirmation Bias

When asking others about decisions they've made, ignore editorializing and focus on details. Ask fact-based questions like, "Can you do X?" or "What would happen if Y?"

Most people look for evidence to confirm that past decisions they made were the right decisions. *Confirmation bias* makes it hard to sort fact from editorializing when asking questions, so try to focus on just the facts.

Opportunity Cost

What else could you do with your time rather than pursuing an opportunity?

How long does it typically take from start to finish? How many hours every week does it take? Will you have to travel to close it? Can you juggle your current work obligations while pursuing it? If not, what will you have to cut?

Get a clear and updated model of what it takes to successfully close the opportunity you want to pursue. There are two ways to mitigate opportunity cost before and while pursuing opportunities:

1. **Talk to others who pursued this opportunity.** Unless an opportunity is truly unique to you, other people have a better model of what it takes to close the opportunity than you do. Talk to them. Find them on social media platforms like LinkedIn and Facebook. Cold email them. Follow the model for landing advisors from Chapter 2.
2. **Make a plan and stick to it.** Make a plan for pursuing an opportunity that takes into account the fact that you have other responsibilities while handling the opportunity. Build out a weekly ROK plan and assign Task Times for pursuing the opportunity. Factor in additional time for unknown unknowns. Don't sacrifice success at your work for the sake of pursuing new opportunities.

Consider Strategic Opportunities

In *select* cases, pursue high-risk, high-reward opportunities (Figure 6.6). These should be pursued *strategically*. Do they get you closer to your long-term goals, based on your Ambition Map?

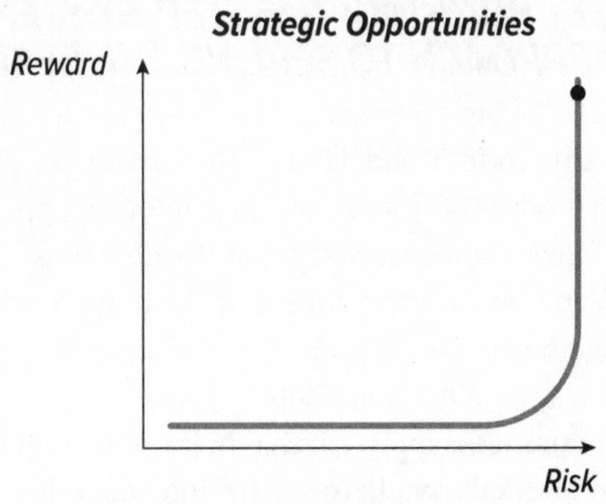

FIGURE 6.6 Strategic opportunities have high risk but also high reward. Pursue these as a conscientious effort to achieve your long-term goals.

Quitting your job, moving across the country, and cashing in your savings to build a startup is a high-risk, high-reward opportunity (Table 6.1). Doing this for low payoff *relative to your career goals* is reckless. Doing this because your career goals include launching a high-growth startup and you believe you found "the idea" is strategic.

	HIGH RISK	LOW RISK
HIGH REWARD	**Strategic Opportunities.** Pursue with a heavy focus on success when it works into your Ambition Map.	**Asymmetric Opportunities.** Pursue unless you have good reason not to.
LOW REWARD	**Reckless Opportunities.** Don't pursue.	**False Opportunities.** Ignore.

TABLE 6.1 The Opportunity Matrix. Download your own template at zakslayback.com/book/oppmatrix.

If you're unsure whether an opportunity is strategic or reckless, get a clearer idea of your goals and revisit your Ambition Map.

GET PITCHING: THE STEP-BY-STEP APPROACH TO SEALING THE DEAL

You've built your brand and landed the chance to pitch yourself for a strategic opportunity or an asymmetric opportunity. You don't want to take the bureaucratic approach of just filling out an application. You don't want to take a hackish approach of cobbling something together.

You need a systematic approach.

This is a systematic approach that helps you get inside your target's mind, confidently pitch yourself, and make it impossible for someone to tell you, "no thanks."

Can They Pay You?

It's one thing to pitch yourself to somebody who *wants* to pay you, but it's another if that person doesn't have the funds to make that a reality. Always confirm that your target *can* pay you.

It's tempting to pursue small businesses and startups for new opportunities. Their decision makers are relatively easy to access, and they have few parameters on what they can say yes or no to.

But they also tend to be less willing to pay.

The sweet spot for any opportunity is with a target whose decision makers you have networked with and who can pay you. The more you can build relationships with established organizations, firms, and individuals with steady cash flow, the better your chances of getting paid.

Make It Impossible to Say No

The work of an irresistible pitch comes long before the pitch is actually made. Your positioning disqualifies most opportunities that wouldn't be a great fit for you. Your network should connect you with the people who are willing to listen to what you bring to the table.

The *wrong* approach to landing a new opportunity is to approach targets and ask them, "What can I do to help you?" Just like in sending open-ended emails, this is cognitively taxing for the person on the other side of the question and doesn't give the target anything to go off. Even though you *think* you're being helpful and friendly, you're negatively signaling an inability to be useful.

The *right* approach involves doing research on the target opportunity before even making the pitch. Just like with landing a mentor, you want to figure out what gaps you can close and exactly how you can do that. If you do this properly, your targets will feel like you're reading their minds. Make it hard for them to say no.

Ethical Mind-Reading

Mind-reading isn't just for psychics and crazed cult leaders. Great salespeople and marketers are mind-readers. They *know* when they make a pitch to *the right people* that they'll get targets to bite.

Their secret? They talk to their *right people.* And they listen.

They listen to the problems their right people face. They listen to the words they use. They listen to the emotions they describe. They listen to how these right people describe their problems. And they only make a pitch when they know their product can actually serve the right people.

The bar is low. So few people take an approach of, "Let me hear your problems and then solve them," when pitching themselves for new opportunities. Talk to your targets. Listen to them. Understand their problems. And figure out not just how you can solve those problems for them but also how you can frame solving those problems *using the same words they use.*

Incentive Mapping

Illustrate what problems others have and how you can solve them through an exercise called *incentive mapping*.

While listening to the people you want to pitch, ask yourself, "What do they want to achieve? What do they want to avoid?" Better yet—ask them. Ask them why they're stressed about a big deadline, why they need to close more deals, or why they want to find a big story to cover.

Then, write down their *exact* words in one of two columns. If they want to *avoid* an outcome, write what they said in an "avoid" column. If they want to *achieve* an outcome, write what they said in an "achieve" column (Table 6.2).

ACHIEVE	AVOID

TABLE 6.2 Incentive Mapping. When pitching yourself for an opportunity, get clear on what incentives the person(s) you're pitching faces. What language do they use to describe what they want and don't want? Download your own template at zakslayback.com/book/incentivemapping.

This illustrates what issues they face and how you can help them—both as a professional and as a person.

For example, you may pitch a middle manager. While talking to him, you realize he doesn't want to look bad in front of his boss. So, if you frame a pitch in terms of how it might make him look good in front of his boss, you'll read his mind.

While building relationships and talking to your right people, look for language that indicates expectations. People feel resentful and frustrated when expectations get violated. They feel grateful when others go above and beyond expectations. If they express feelings of guilt, frustration, resentment, or indignation, those are telltale signs of expectations being violated.

Craft Your Pitch

Once you have an idea of what, exactly, your right people feel and what problems they need solved, let them know that you're the person to solve those problems.

Set an Outcome and Clear Expectations

Set an outcome and expectations that are easy for you to hit but would still solve your right person's problems. Don't promise the world if you can't absolutely deliver it. Keep expectations low so that, should you not exceed them, you at least don't burn your relationship and create resentment. Underpromise so you can overdeliver.

Be Specific in Your Pitch—Use Incentive Maps

Don't simply tell them, "I can solve problems for you." Tell them, "I can solve *this specific* problem for you, with the language you described. In fact, I already developed a plan for how I can do that. And solving this problem will help you avoid these outcomes and achieve these outcomes."

Don't Use Jargon

Use words real people use. Don't use jargon. Nobody "utilizes" anything. "Synergy" is only used by out-of-touch HR people. And nobody is "activated" by marketing.

The right people want results. They want interesting stories that keep readers coming back. They want happy employees. They want users to keep using their app every day. They want to feel confident about their decisions.

That's all you have to say in your initial pitch.

Once you've confirmed interest, send along your detailed explanation of how you'll create that outcome for them. Don't worry too much about the details of the explanation. The purpose of sending it along is to signal your ability to get work done and get it done well. The specific plan of action comes later. Details change moment to moment.

Use Risk Reversal

At any offer or pitch, people look for the risks. Each risk is a chance for them to say, "no thanks." Drastically reduce the chances of your right people saying no through risk reversal.

The biggest risks associated with pitches like this are loss of time, money, and an exit option.

Reverse these in your pitch through the following:

- **Success stories and social proof.** Showing that others trusted you to do similar work helps reverse the risk of losing time and money working with you. Collect endorsements that highlight how easy it is to work with you. These, combined with your detailed plan of attack, reduce the risk of losing time by working with you.
- **Trial period or refund.** Offer to start on a trial period (or in the case of offering a product, offer a refund window). This works particularly well when pitching yourself for your dream job. Let the right people know that you'll work to create the result you pitched them for 30, 60, or 90 days. If they aren't happy when that time ends, they're under no obligation to keep working with you. This conveys confidence and a belief in what you have to offer. It's rare that you'll do such a poor job that you'll actually get a refund request. If you take a trial period approach, set *clear* expectations on what success looks like and what your right people commit to when you succeed.

Charge What You're Worth

Don't expect others to pay you what you think you're worth without you asking.

How much you charge is a function of your positioning, your market, and your experience. If you're just entering a market for the first time, you may choose to work for free. If you're positioned as an elite or high-end employee, entrepreneur, creator, or maker, quote toward the top of your market.

If you're just starting out, start your pricing relatively low (based on your market; if pitching yourself for a job, use glassdoor.com or salary.com) and quickly raise your rates with experience, success stories, a network, and social capital. It's easier to start too low and quickly raise prices than it is to start high and slash prices. Plus, your goal here is to get your foot in the door and prove your worth.

Make Yourself Irreplaceable

Focus on delivering results. Deliver your promised results ahead of schedule, in greater detail than offered, and with focus on generating the outcome your right people want.

Your goal here should be to not just meet expectations but to exceed them. You can actually invert power dynamics and make the people you want to work with grateful to you. You do this through going above and beyond what is expected of you and people in your role.

By focusing on outcome delivery and exceeding expectations, you present an opportunity to the person you're pitching: either continue working with you past your trial period (and potentially compensate you better to retain you) or go through the arduous process of replacing you.

If You Don't Ask, You Don't Get

Once you've delivered results, if your right people haven't already told you they intend to keep working with you, *ask*. Tell them that you'd like to continue working with them and quote them a price to keep working together.

Unless your expectations and their expectations are way off base, they'll jump on the chance to keep working with you.

HOW TO BUILD A WORLD-CLASS NETWORK . . . AND FLOOD YOURSELF WITH AMAZING OPPORTUNITIES (PART 2)

AJ followed a process like this once he landed his phone calls with Kevin Rose and the team at Oak (see Part 1 in Chapter 5).

AJ knew his skills and positioning well enough to make a compelling first pitch to Kevin. He could help Kevin and his team drive user engagement and reduce user churn. That was interesting enough to get on the phone with AJ. From there, AJ focused on building trust with Kevin and his team and learning their expectations. He pitched them on a big consulting deal. They passed on that because of timing for other projects their team had to do.

Instead of feeling dejected and backing out of the opportunity to work with a superstar, AJ went back to relationship-building mode. He scheduled a trip from San Francisco to Portland to casually meet with Kevin and the team over coffee.

Be Sure to Get Face Time

Getting face time with your right people gives you a distinct advantage in networking. For high-value opportunities, consider making a "planned" trip to wherever your right people are.

Find a few days that you can go to their city if you confirm a meeting. Before booking travel, send them an email telling them you plan on visiting for those days and would like to meet while you're in town. If they confirm, book the trip. If they don't, don't book the trip.

AJ met Kevin and the team over lunch and dinner, discussed their goals for the coming months and year, and immediately jumped in on how he could help them achieve those goals. He extended his trip through the weekend to outline a plan of action and summarize takeaways from their conversations.

Before leaving, he had a 20-page summary and plan of action that the entire team could use. He made a point to be quick in his communication, slash his prices for the chance to work with this team, and focus on what *they* needed.

"I never even asked him if drafting a 20-page report summarizing our findings at the end was something he wanted," AJ told me after reviewing what happened. "I just intuited, based off our conversations, that this is what would be most useful for him in the long run. But he ended up loving it and sharing it with the whole team this fall . . . and they all said how helpful it was for them to inform their own jobs."

While I was working on the final draft of this book, AJ gave me an unexpected call.

"Oak just offered me an opportunity to work directly with them," he told me.

"This sounds like your dream opportunity," I told him. I wasn't surprised. AJ signaled all the right traits, and the team would be foolish to *not* work with him. Even though he was trying to land a freelance opportunity, he brought his dream opportunity to him.

"It pretty much is," he replied.

Oak eventually pivoted from its initial plans, and AJ used the opportunity to pitch himself for *even more dream opportunities* with people from Kevin's world-class network. AJ had proven himself to a mentor and advisor with a world-class network. By virtue of that, he gained trust and credibility with some of the top minds in the technology and mindfulness spaces. Instead of viewing his career through a box-checking or hack lens, he viewed every step of the way as a chance to identify and close even better opportunities.

AJ's story illustrates the power of carefully crafting your brand and your positioning, mindfully building a network, and pitching yourself. While he's an extraordinarily hard worker and driven to accomplish his goals, he's not unique. Anybody can set up for opportunities in the way he did. You just have to understand who your right people are, what their problems are, and how you can help them.

KEY TAKEAWAYS

- **Don't wait** until you *need* opportunities to pitch yourself for them.
- Unless you have good reason not to, **always work on closing an asymmetric opportunity**. This gives you negotiating leverage, keeps your pitching skills sharp, and gives you feedback on what you need to improve.
- **Make it impossible for the right people to tell you no** by speaking to their pain points, reversing their risk, exceeding their expectations, and making it more costly for them to say no.

ACTION ITEMS

1. Download the Opportunity Matrix at zakslayback.com/book/oppmatrix.
2. Identify at least three asymmetric opportunities you can pursue.
3. Write down a list of the intangible rewards you'd get and the intangible risks you'd face.
4. Rank-order these opportunities based on rewards.
5. Develop a plan for closing your top asymmetric opportunity.
6. Identify at least one reckless opportunity and one false opportunity. Ignore these.
7. Identify one strategic opportunity to pursue in the future. Are you in a position to pitch yourself for it now? If not, what do you need to do to get there?

CONCLUSION

Putting It All Together

This is a book about how to create opportunities for yourself. It's a book about how to think *systematically* about your career. And it's a book you can return to time and time again.

The process of **Focus–Learn–Execute–Signal–Connect–Close** works whether you're just starting a new career, trying to get to a new stage in your job, or looking to launch your own business (Figure I.1). I've seen it work with everybody from serial startup entrepreneurs and seasoned executives to recent graduates and homeschool moms looking to get back into the workplace. I've been fortunate to see these concepts in my work as a career development writer and in my work in the venture capital world.

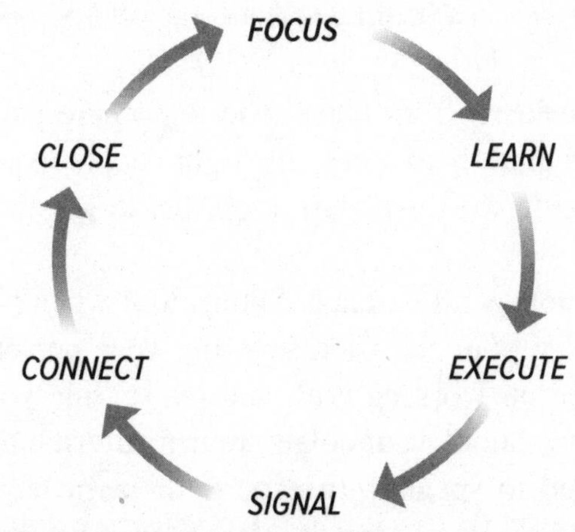

FIGURE I.1 The Opportunity Machine. Focus, Learn, Execute, Signal, Connect, and Close to create new career opportunities.

What matters is understanding where you are and where you want to go. As you gain experience in a new stage of your career, the value of your time increases. It's just not worth your time to work on tasks that aren't related to your job. *But the value of your time is still worth less* than that of where you'll be in the future (Figure C.1).

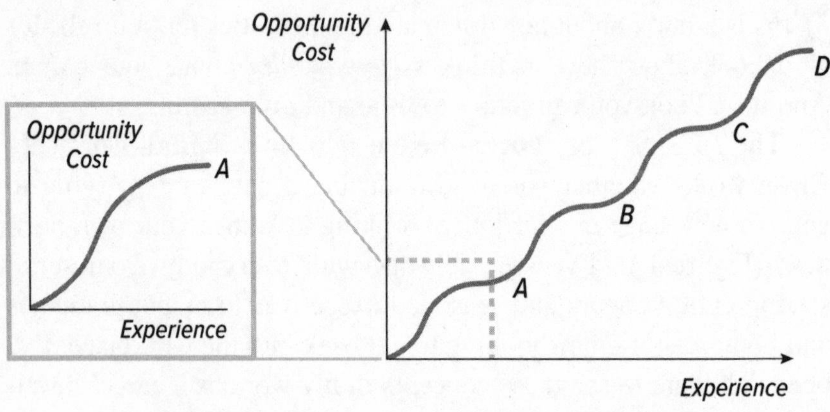

FIGURE C.1 Your opportunity cost is low *relative to* the new stage of your career you want to unleash. You can always leverage your low opportunity cost to learn from somebody more experienced and skilled than yourself.

Use that to learn from those who are where you want to be. Use that to signal to them and to the right people that you're somebody they want to work with. And use that to get ahead, time and time again.

Use this book as a reference. Return to it when you face questions of building your network, growing your personal brand, or pitching people on working with you. Next time you need to sit down and think about your goals, return to Ambition Mapping. When you need to speak with experts or learn tacit knowledge, return to your Cabinet of Models. Next time you face a big project and feel overwhelmed, apply ROK to your week.

As you apply these concepts, I'd love to hear from you. Send me an email at zak.slayback@getaheadlabs.com telling me about your career goals and what you took from this book.

BIBLIOGRAPHY AND FURTHER READING

Please visit zakslayback.com/book/reading for detailed explanation for how each of these books influenced every chapter.

Chapter 1

Branden, Nathaniel. *The Six Pillars of Self-Esteem*. New York: Bantam, 1994.

Branden, Nathaniel. *Self-Esteem at Work: How Confident People Make Powerful Companies*. San Francisco, CA: Jossey-Bass, 1998.

Branden, Nathaniel. *Honoring the Self: Self-Esteem and Personal Transformation*. New York: Bantam, 2004.

Girard, René. *I See Satan Fall Like Lightning*. Ossining, NY: Orbis Books, 2001.

Newport, Cal. *So Good They Can't Ignore You: Why Skills Trump Passion in the Quest for Work You Love*. London: Piatkus Books, 2016.

Peterson, Jordan B. *Maps of Meaning: The Architecture of Belief*. New York: Routledge, 1999.

Taleb, Nassim Nicholas. *Antifragile: Things That Gain from Disorder*. New York: Random House, 2016.

Tavris, Carol, and Elliot Aronson. *Mistakes Were Made (but Not by Me): Why We Justify Foolish Beliefs, Bad Decisions, and Hurtful Acts*. London: Pinter & Martin, 2016.

Thiel, Peter, and Masters, Blake. *Zero to One: Notes on Startups, or How to Build the Future*. New York: Currency, 2014.

Chapter 2

Beck, Molly. *Reach Out: The Simple Strategy You Need to Expand Your Network and Increase Your Influence.* New York: McGraw-Hill, 2018.

Chapter 3

Allen, David. *Getting Things Done: The Art of Stress-Free Productivity.* New York: Viking, 2001.

Clear, James. *Atomic Habits: An Easy & Proven Way to Build Good Habits & Break Bad Ones*, New York: Avery, 2018

Newport, Cal. *Deep Work: Rules for Focused Success in a Distracted World.* London: Piatkus, 2016.

Selk, Jason, Tom Bartow, and Matthew Rudy. *Organize Tomorrow Today: 8 Ways to Retrain Your Mind to Optimize Performance at Work and in Life.* Boston, MA: Da Capo, 2016.

Chapter 4

Abraham, Jay. *Getting Everything You Can Out of All You've Got: 21 Ways You Can Out-Think, Out-Perform, and Out-Earn the Competition*, New York: St. Martin's Griffin, 2001.

Ferriss, Timothy. *The 4-Hour Workweek: Escape 9–5, Live Anywhere, and Join the New Rich.* New York: Harmony Books, 2012.

Holiday, Ryan. *Trust Me, I'm Lying: Confessions of a Media Manipulator.* New York: Profile Books. 2018.

Chapter 5

Carnegie, Dale. *How to Win Friends & Influence People.* New York: Pocket Books, 2007.

Ferrazzi, Keith, and Tahl Raz. *Never Eat Alone, Expanded and Updated: And Other Secrets to Success, One Relationship at a Time.* Crown Business, 2014.

Chapter 6

Abraham, Jay. *Getting Everything You Can Out of All You've Got: 21 Ways You Can Out-Think, Out-Perform, and Out-Earn the Competition*, New York: St. Martin's Griffin, 2001.

Adams, Scott. *How to Fail at Almost Everything and Still Win Big: Kind of the Story of My Life*. New York: Portfolio/Penguin, 2014.

Bell, Macalester. *Hard Feelings: The Moral Psychology of Contempt*. New York: Oxford University Press, 2013.

Dawson, Roger. *Secrets of Power Negotiating, 15th Anniversary Edition: Inside Secrets from a Master Negotiator*. Newburyport: Weiser, 2010.

Klaff, Oren. *Pitch Anything: An Innovative Method for Presenting, Persuading and Winning the Deal*. New York: McGraw-Hill, 2011.

Ury, William. *Getting Past No: Negotiating in Difficult Situations*. New York: Bantam Books, 2007.

Voss, Chris. *Never Split the Difference: Negotiating as If Your Life Depended on It*. New York: Random House Business, 2017.

INDEX

ABOUT THE AUTHOR

Photo by Hannah Phillips

Zak Slayback is a career expert, writer, and venture capital professional. He writes at ZakSlayback.com and creates career development material at GetAheadLabs.com. He's a principal at 1517 Fund (1517fund.com), a venture capital fund that invests in technology companies run by young founders working outside of tracked institutions like academia.

His writing and strategies have been featured in *Fast Company*, *The Muse*, *Newsweek*, *The Christian Science Monitor*, and the *New York Observer*, among others. He's a regular speaker to student groups, entrepreneur groups, and corporations looking to learn more about building a world-class network and landing new professional opportunities.

He was previously the Director of Business Development for a talent development startup and a researcher at the University of Pennsylvania.

You can read more of his writing and join his newsletter at ZakSlayback.com.